Occupation as the
Key to Change

Occupation as the Key to Change

A collection of stories

and suggestions illustrating

the power of occupation

Peter M. Talty, MS, OTR/L

Professor Emeritus of Occupational Therapy

Keuka College

Keuka Park, New York

authorHOUSE®

AuthorHouse™
1663 Liberty Drive
Bloomington, IN 47403
www.authorhouse.com
Phone: 1-800-839-8640

Published by AuthorHouse   08/15/2012

ISBN: 978-1-4772-5921-4 (sc)
ISBN: 978-1-4772-5922-1 (e)

Library of Congress Control Number: 2012914563

Contents

Preface

Professor Peter Talty has provided a collection of exceptional stories that have served and will continue to serve as teaching tools for students and professionals. Story telling is an essential part of developing competent professionals. In theoretical terms, storytelling can be described as using narrative to teach tacit professional knowledge and skills within the context of an individual's environment. The art of using storytelling as a teaching tool provides knowledge beyond books and tests. Storytelling teaches professional skills beyond words in terms of communication skills and the use of a person's current situation for enhancing their quality of life. The value of these stories cannot be measured. Professor Talty's story contributions reflect his advanced teaching and clinical skills relating to his knowledge, passion, and dedication to lifelong learning. I am proud to be among the colleagues that have worked and learned from Professor Talty and thank him for his dedication to the profession.

Vicki Smith Ed.D, MBA, OTR/L
Professor and Chair of Occupational Therapy
Keuka College
Keuka Park, NY 14478

Author's Note

"I wish it need not have happened in my time," said Frodo.

"So do I," said Gandalf, "and so do all who live to see such times. But that is not for them to decide. All we have to decide is what to do with the time that is given us."

J.R.R. Tolkien, *The Fellowship of the Ring*

In my over forty years of practice as an occupational therapist and educator I have met many Frodos. I purposely avoided being a Gandalf; choosing instead to ask questions and avoid giving advice. Although I often could clearly see what the person needed to do to extricate themselves from an "it" like Frodo's, I refrained from directing them to what I saw as the needed resolution. I felt that people know their own situations best, and have far more knowledge of available resources than I in solving their problems. This is true of all people whether they be patients, students, friends, or family. Asking key questions at opportune times can lead to insight and action. The action I speak of is the engagement in a valued activity or occupation that results in learning and subsequent change.

What each person chooses to do with their time dictates certain results. Engagement in meaningful activities or occupations can be the key to change. Ideally, patients practice skills and carry out exercises to enable them to lead satisfying and independent lives. Also ideally, students study and acquire knowledge and skills to become licensed occupational therapists. But, do patients, students, and people in general change and adapt so fluidly? Sometimes, but usually with large challenges and those replete with emotion the change may not be fluid at all. It may even be calamitous. That is where the right occupation at the right time can make the difference.

I have had the opportunity to observe and experience this process of engagement in occupations leading to change, and have discovered some strategies that facilitate people adapting and learning. I have put forth some stories here that illustrate these strategies in action. The stories are my personal experiences, and since they involve patients and students going through difficult situations I have done everything I could to safeguard their privacy. Names and locales that are mentioned are all fictitious.

Most people generate their own change and do not need another person whether it is an OT or just a good friend to do it. But, this book is not about these people. It is about those whose engagement in activities was without meaning and without the desired results. Contained within these stories are keys to change using occupations and various approaches that caused people, including myself, to change and adapt. My goal is not to make readers into Gandalfs, but to help the Frodos resolve their own situations leading to a better life as they perceive it.

Peter Talty

Acknowledgements

Without the support, guidance, and encouragement of my wife Janice and one of my students, Michelle York, this book would never have been written. I always thought I should write a book, and my students and family members have repeatedly encouraged me to do so. But, I chose to do other things with my time, and not until Michelle said she would help me with it did I seriously consider taking on the task. Michelle is an outstanding occupational therapy student who was going through her senior year at Keuka College at the time we began talking about this book. Her prior background in journalism proved invaluable as she edited my work and made excellent suggestions. Her clear and direct feedback definitely made this a far better book than I could have ever produced alone.

Janice, my wife of almost 47 years has always understood my commitment to OT and was accustomed to making adjustments in order for me to focus on whatever related challenge I decided to take on. This book was that latest challenge. She understood, as she always did, that I had to work on the book even during our month of vacation in Florida and beyond. There was never any complaining, and in fact she was always encouraging. Also, her feedback was so helpful whenever I would share my writing with her. It was her clear and objective thinking that strengthened each edition of the book.

I must also recognize the patients, students, friends, and family that I have interacted with over the years. Their willingness to view their situations or challenges in a different way, and to immerse themselves in a beneficial occupation provided the substance for this book. Their struggles, successes, and even failures provided direct evidence of the power of occupation to effect change. I was privileged to be a witness to this process.

To Janice, Michelle and all those who used occupation to effect change in their lives I am very grateful, and know absolutely that this book is theirs as well as mine.

Peter Talty

Part I:

The making of a change agent

Change Agent:

1. *A role in which communication skills, education, and other resources are applied to help a client adjust to changes caused by illness or disability.*

2. *A role to help members of organizations adapt to organizational change or to create organizational change.*
   Mosby's Medical Dictionary, 8th edition. 2009, Elsevier.

Occupation:
"…. Occupation, a collection of activities that people use to fill their time and give life meaning, is organized around roles or in terms of activities of daily living, work and productive activities, or pleasure, for survival, for necessity, and for their personal meaning. It is the individualized, unique combination of activities that comprises an individual's occupations."

American Journal of Occupational Therapy, 1997
Nov-Dec 51 (10) 864-6.
Hinojosa J, Kramer P.

1. Looking back .... way, way back

"What is opportunity, and when does it knock? It never knocks. You can wait a whole lifetime, listening, hoping, and you will hear no knocking. None at all. You are opportunity, and you must knock on the door leading to your destiny. You prepare yourself to recognize opportunity, to pursue and seize opportunity as you develop the strength of your personality, and build a self-image with which you are able to live with your self-respect alive and growing."
Maxwell Maltz (1899-1975)
American cosmetic surgeon and author of Psycho-Cybernetics

It is well known that what we become has roots in our early life experience. I, like most people, can trace the remnants of my sense of self back through time. Reflecting on my own experiences including the role occupation played in my life has been very informative and inspirational. I describe these events in an effort to demonstrate that change within us is directly related to change within our environments, coupled with a good amount of reflection and introspection. Thus, the reciprocal and dynamic aspects of internal and external change are integral to life, and occupation is a powerful mediator of this process.

Like many driven people I was not always driving in the right direction or at the most prudent speed for conditions. If having crazy times in one's life gives one a unique vantage point, then I must be a wizard.

My parents were overwhelmed with too many children too early in their lives, and my father lacked the focus to get his growing family into a secure place in the world. Alcohol took this intelligent man in a sad direction and contributed to his early death at age 54. He missed a lot in life, and we missed knowing a lot about him. He was certainly not an agent of change; rather he was a often a victim of the changes swirling about him. His chosen occupations did not enable him to seize control of his and his family's lives, but he did provide an inadvertent message to us all that his was not the path to follow in life.

Conversely, my mother's positive attitude is the reason I can deal with adversity fairly well today. Her frequent saying when faced with a crisis was that we should "get the facts before we react" is one of my most valued perspectives when dealing with difficult situations or crises. She always hoped and dreamed that things would get better, but was not able to get my father to focus on job, family, and security in order to bring this about. He was distracted by the bright lights and fun he found in bars. This made for a difficult childhood for us all, but we all eventually rose above it to become solid workers, family-oriented, and good citizens.

We remain close today and have been each other's support and inspiration throughout the years. We also each found solid spouses that helped us each build the home and family life we lacked as kids. Our occupations, both career and interest-wise, supported and enriched our lives. Before I became an OT I did not appreciate how powerful the kinds of activities or occupations we elect to engage in support or diminish one's health, well-being, and sense of self.

Because we did not have much growing up I was always on the alert to seize opportunities. My earliest recollection of this occurred when I was 7 years old. It was at a time when I desperately wanted to earn money to buy a baseball glove, comic books, etc. But with no allowance, being too young to babysit and too small to cut lawns (I was puny then) my prospects were very limited.

I figured out that what I needed to do was to get a newspaper-delivery route. That would be my ticket to prosperity (I was grandiose even then). However, there was a large obstacle in my way: You had to be at least 12 years old. Then, an opportunity appeared.

It was during a baseball game of older boys in the park that I got my chance. I was too young to play and was just hanging around when I heard that "Spike" was greatly upsetting his teammates by announcing that he would have to leave the game to deliver his afternoon newspapers. His team knew that they would probably lose this close game without him. So, I rushed into the middle of the discussion and yelled: "I'll get your papers for you Spike and you can keep on playing. By the time I get back the game will be over, and I can help you deliver your papers."

His team thought it was a great idea and pressured Spike into letting me do it. So, off I went. I don't remember if they won the game or not. I was too wrapped up in my excitement of delivering newspapers just like a big kid. I offered to help him every day on his six-day route, and he agreed to pay me twenty-five cents per day. Now I really was on my way to prosperity!

I continued on my quest to make money and graduated to my own small paper route that was in my brother's name because I was still too young. It was a weekly flyer of sales for local stores that I was supposed to deliver to every house in my area. No one seemed interested in getting this paper, so I decided to not deliver them but still I still accepted the $2.00 a week in payment. My mother rolled and put rubber bands on the flyers each Tuesday night and I would dump them either into a nearby field or off a bridge into the Cazenovia Creek before their Thursday delivery time.

After a few weeks, that accumulation in the field caught the eye of my older sister who investigated and exposed my scam to my mother. She made me give up the route. What did I learn from this dumb caper? I learned that I was both stupid and deceitful. Not good building blocks for adulthood or a change agent. Sixty years after this awful venture, the guilt still resonates.

But I also learned early on that my best assets were my work ethic and perseverance. My work ethic came from my sister Sue who was 13 years older than me. I spent a lot of time with her as an adolescent helping her by babysitting my niece and doing housework. I enjoyed hearing her view of the world and people. She was bright, funny, assertive, organized, hard-working, and perceptive. It was from her that I learned how to anticipate consequences and to plan for adversity. She could have been anything in life, but was burdened with our family's troubles that sapped her drive over the years.

I had the opportunity to apply my sister's work ethic when I became a pinsetter in a bowling alley at age 13. Back in the 1950s, bowling had become very popular and almost all of the bowling alleys had converted to the automatic pinsetters. But there was one antiquated bowling alley near my house that still used men to set the pins up on its 16 lanes after each ball was thrown. This bowling alley used a cadre of homeless men to work the alleys.

Most of them had drinking problems. On the nights they were deemed by the owner to be too drunk to work, I would get my chance. This was never known in advance, and so I and some other boys would wait around to see if we could take their place. The other boys quickly got frustrated with the waiting. As they faded, I kept on waiting—always ready to go in. And it paid off in that I was able to work two or three nights a week. It was hot, dirty, noisy, and hard work. Because this was often on school nights that I worked until 1:00 AM, it was one more reason for me not to work at becoming a good student in high school.

Unfortunately, my emerging sense of drive did not carry over to my schoolwork. I disliked school, fell behind on assignments, did not pay attention, and preferred to mess around. Frequently, I got into fights that I usually lost. I think the teachers kept passing me to either just to get rid of me, or because they thought I had some potential based on my performance on their frequent aptitude and intelligence tests. My teachers and parents were confounded that I could score well on these tests, and yet performed so poorly in my schoolwork. They tried to get me to buckle down, but I was not interested or very motivated about school. This did not come until I experienced life as a high school dropout and went to night school for five years (two to finish high school and three years of college).

Coupled with my drive was a good amount of risk taking that I cannot associate with any family member or adult role model. When I was 11, this risk taking took the form of hopping on freight trains for rides of several hundred miles. When I was a teenager and young adult, this took the form of driving fast, driving drunk and/or high, jumping off cliffs—tempting fate wherever I could. Also, wherever I lived, worked, or played I always sought out the risk takers to accompany me. I found sensible and focused people boring.

Through a recovery program and a higher power, I saw the light on July 25th of 1982. Eventually, my risk-taking led me to explore the outdoors with canoeing, backpacking, and hiking. Professionally, it also enabled me to take jobs and develop the first OT programs in many facilities, and to run my own private practice for ten years which I named *OT Works*.

I was very fortunate that this entire risk taking did not result in death or severe injuries to myself or others, or financial ruin for my family. I also found, my outdoor adventures of canoeing, backpacking, and cycling gave me far more satisfaction.

Another attribute I developed early on was being organized. Even as a kid I was always organized and kept my room neat and my stuff where I could always find it. Unfortunately, my three brothers did not have these same obsessions with structure and control as I, so there were lots of arguments around these issues.

This need for structure and control has helped me tremendously as both an OT and as an educator, but has also often made me crazy because so many elements of my work and life were not able to be controlled. Patients, students, friends, colleagues, and family members all want to control their own lives and destinies (can you imagine?) regardless of the consequences. A good change agent has to restrain the tendency to take control of other people's situations, and I'm still working on that.

Persuading people to take courses of action that they may view as unappealing or not relevant to their situation regardless of how good I think it would be for them is still something I struggle with today. The approach I now use is to never give advice or try to convince anyone to change a direction they have chosen. I do however ask a lot of questions not only in an effort to better understand a person's situation, but to perhaps help them to gain a different perspective on their problem. This comes from the belief that people really know more about their specific situation and resources than anyone else, and that usually they are the best people to solve it. You will see repeated applications of this strategy in some of my upcoming stories.

It seems that no matter what experiences I have, positive or negative, I always gain from them. I reflect and read. I am not big on drawing conclusions based on other people's opinions. The exception of course is when the person is a recognized expert in the area that is related to my interest at a given time. Sometimes I have the experience and then much later read something that gives me that "aha!" feeling. At other times, it's the rich repository of experiences and knowledge that I have gained over the years that helps me to understand current situations and people.

This ability and willingness to reflect on experience no matter how painful has served me well over the years. No one helps me do this better than my wife Janice who I love more today than I did when we married on October 30ᵗʰ 1965. Having a life partner like her has been invaluable. She is far more patient than I, and always sees the best in people. I draw on these attributes of hers on a daily basis, and will do so forever.

This brief autobiography provides some of the underpinnings that aid me as an occupational therapist, educator, and change agent today. You will see traces of these elements in the stories below, and how occupation is really the medium that helps me help others as a change agent.

2. How I Found OT or Did OT Find Me?

"Find something you love to do and you'll never have to work a day in your life."
Harvey Mackay (1932—) Columnist and Author

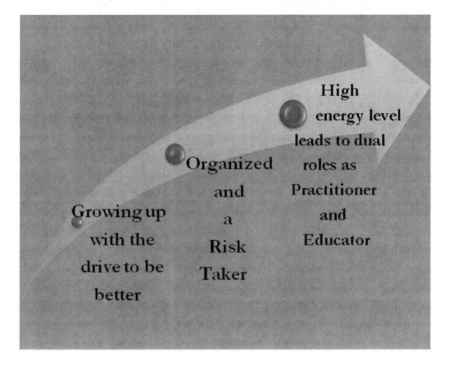

Figure 2-1. The making of a change agent and the factors that contributed to OT as my career choice and eventual roles.

When I first went to college in 1964 I had no idea of what I was going to be. My only knowledge of OT was that it was something some members of my family did while hospitalized in mental health facilities. They made bird houses out of reed, leather moccasins, ceramic coffee mugs, and so forth. If I gave any thought to it at all, it was that OT was just another word for crafts and not an actual profession. I had no idea what OT was or what it was to become. I also of course had no idea that becoming an occupational therapist would be the foundation for my life as a change agent.

My path to OT was not linear. Rather, mine was a circuitous and convoluted route. For example, while in college I read a story about a man who was a high school dropout (like me) who went back to high school, then on to college, and became a social worker. This inspired me to want to do the same, and so I began taking courses along those lines. However, at the time I didn't even realize that there was a difference between a social worker and a caseworker. A friend of my brother's was a caseworker who convinced me to just get a degree in any related field and then I could join him as a caseworker at the Department of Social Services or what was colloquially known as the *Welfare Department*. I really liked the idea of helping people and found his stories of his work interesting and this formed a vision to pursue. The degree that seemed most applicable and most interesting to me at the same time was either sociology or psychology, so I planned my courses in order to complete a degree in one of these majors. As I think back, I realized that throughout five years of undergraduate work and four changes in majors I never consulted an academic advisor. I just studied the college catalog and did what it said to do. This may have been a mistake because I may have been able to shorten my journey to the OT profession.

After I had taken 30 hours of psychology and 15 hours of Sociology I decided to get my degree in anthropology instead. The social worker/caseworker career was no longer attractive to me. At that time I was envisioning myself completing a doctorate in anthropology and then living with some tribal group and doing ethnographic research to learn about their culture. However, I got married and two years later our son was born, so my anthropology degree was not going to work out the way I had planned. Thus, it was in this state of academic angst that I accidently discovered OT. I was waiting to go into one of my anthropology classes, and noticed a bulletin board with OT information on it and some brochures. In scanning the requirements I saw that they required 27 hours of psychology (I had 30), two biology courses, sociology, a foreign language, and a bunch of other courses that I already had taken. I elected to skip my class and walk down the hall to the OT Department and check out changing my major to OT. Unlike today, there weren't a lot of people who knew about OT or were very interested in it as a major, so they were very receptive to my inquiries. Even though it was a five year program at that time (four years of classroom courses and three Level II Fieldwork experiences of three months each) I was not deterred.

I took all the information home and my wife and I discussed the pros and cons of making the shift to OT. If I stayed in anthropology, I would have my bachelor's degree in a year and a half, but still have the doctorate to complete. By switching to OT it would take me two and a half additional years including the Fieldwork experiences to earn my OT degree. Because the job prospects were far better for OT than anthropology and I had a family to support I decided to be practical and become an OT.

The changing of majors had a great impact on our lives because now I would have to find a new full-time job, and it would have to be a night job. Up to this point I had been able to work full-time days as a janitor in a grammar school while finishing high school and completing 75 credits of college credit at night. However, OT was only offered in a day school format, and the first course (Gross Anatomy) started in six weeks. I contacted a friend of our family's who had spent several years working in a local steel plant; to see if he might be able to help me get a night job there. He responded favorably to my request, and instructed me as to what to say when I went to the steel plant's employment office. The plant was doing some hiring, but not to a large extent, and there must have been forty men filling out applications. It turned out that the friend of my family had great influence and I was hired. I was assigned to a menial job of shoveling steel scrap out from under large lathe machines, and intermittently working as a "Hooker" (not that kind) where I hooked large cables on to massive steel rolls that were moved by an overhead crane to other parts of the mill. It was hot, boring, dangerous, and dirty work, but it allowed me to enter the OT program as a full-time OT student and support my family.

At the steel plant I found myself in a difficult situation in that the men in the department to which I was assigned had a negative attitude towards college students. While other night workers were allowed to sleep for about two or three hours on the job, I was not. Other Hookers could sleep in between "lifts" or roll changes along

11

with the crane operator, but in between lifts they made me climb back under the giant lathe machines and shovel out the steel scraps. These were difficult days and nights because at the same time I was taking Gross Anatomy. This was a five-day a week course that met from 8:30 to 12:30 including the human dissection in the lab. There was so much to learn and do that most people (especially me) had to go back into the lab after lunch for further dissection and memorization. I don't know how but I survived this grueling six week course and passed. I then had a month off from college, and so being able to sleep more with only my steel plant job to do was like heaven.

Then came the fall and I was fully engaged in the full OT junior curriculum while continuing to work all night at the steel plant. I did this routine of eight hours of work at the steel plant, full-time OT school, and being a husband and father all on 4 or 5 hours of sleep for another semester. Then a wonderful thing happened. One day when I reported to work I was told to go to a different department and report to a man I did not know, but he knew of me or I should say of my family.

This man had grown up with my mother and was now in a very high position and responsible for some major operations at the plant. When I went to see him he was very gracious and respectful; things that I had not experienced at the steel plant before. He had seen my name some place and had found out that I was going to college. This impressed him and coupled with the connection with my mother we became" buddies". He told me that he thought it was great that I was putting myself through college and that he was going to help me. The help came in the form of being assigned an office job as a clerk at night where I could do some simple recording of data (by hand, no computers in those days), and have the office to myself. There were no supervisors of the office at night and the plant supervisors had no control over me. Thanks to this miraculous arrangement I was able to do the data entry work for about three or four hours, but then I could study or sleep! I was in heaven! Because I had accustomed myself to sleeping just 4 or 5 hours a night I was able to function fine in OT school and even have time for my family. This limited need for sleep continues today and has enabled me to accomplish a lot in my waking hours as a change agent and more, lots more.

My good fortune continued in that for my senior year I was awarded a scholarship, and coupled with a combination of intermittent part-time jobs ("Page" in a hospital's medical library, summons-server, pizza-deliverer, ice cream truck sales-driver, etc) I was thus able to quit the steel plant! I was also able to get stipends and thus be paid for my Level II Fieldworks which seldom happens today. So, on December 1st of 1969 I had completed all requirements for my B.S. in OT and started my first job. I took the Certification exam a month later, passed, and thus became an OTR.

Without my wife's support and encouragement, and the help of some key people I would not have been able to become an OT. My wife was the anchor that kept our home going and got our family established. Also, without the man who first got me the job in the steel plant and then the other man who befriended me and got me the office job I doubt I could have completed the OT program.

OT has proved an excellent fit for my personality for a number of reasons. I love the diversity in this profession. It amazes me to reflect back on how the profession has matured and flourished as did I. I have had the opportunity to be a practitioner in rehabilitation, schools, developmental disabilities, hand therapy, ergonomics, acute care hospitals, mental health, chemical dependency, home health, hospice, and skilled nursing facilities. This diverse clinical background, coupled with my completing my Master's in Health Science Education, has enabled me to have success as a professor and teacher of OT. To have this diversity of jobs without having to go back to school to become something else just shows what a great field OT has become.

I was also able to become a manager of several OT programs, establish a private practice, become involved in the OT organizations at the local, state, and national levels where a whole other level of learning and skill was required. Becoming an educator was a path I had not considered taking that worked out quite well. In summary, if there is one thing that I learned from all my jobs and life experiences it is that patients, students, and employees all have something in common: everyone wants to become something greater than they are, and helping them achieve it has been very rewarding. Being a change agent has been the culmination of all of my education and experience. As a change agent I have helped students learn and grow, helped patients acquire skills and knowledge that helped them overcome obstacles, and helped family members and friends master challenging situations. All of this was achieved not just by me; but through my knowledge of the effective use of occupation as the vehicle of change.

Part II:

Tools of Change

"One of the greatest and simplest tools for learning more and growing is doing more".
Washington Irving (1783-1859)
American Writer

3. Never underestimate the power of the relationship

"The meeting of two personalities is like the contact of two chemical substances: if there is any reaction, both are transformed."
Carl G. Jung (1875-1961)
Swiss psychologist and psychiatrist

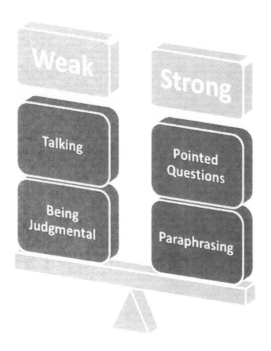

Figure 3-1. The factors that "build bridges" and provide the basis for change.

When I first started working in occupational therapy in 1970, the OT practice settings in those days had the pace of a minor-league baseball game—short, infrequent bursts of action, when clients would arrive for treatment, interspersed with long pauses. We had time—time to get to know the person behind the diagnosis and understand the anguish they were often feeling.

Today, many OT practice settings, by financial necessity, often have the pace of a hockey game. Therapists work frenetically as they move their clients through a set of precise, fast-paced procedures while hoping they don't skid into each other or slip up. It is an imperfect setting for treating patients. Yet, this is the reality in the modern health-care system, and OTs have adapted quite well to this demanding environment.

The trade-off for time is that now therapists have more education and technology available as compared to 40 years ago. Yet, the importance of building a relationship with the client has not diminished over the decades. However, the process of helping clients change cannot occur until the therapist forges a bridge of trust and respect. Not easy to do with large caseloads and short lengths of stay.

However, if we foster an open and compassionate way of responding we can build a relationship from the moment we meet our patients. We start by looking at their eyes, sometimes before we look at their chart, eliciting their stories, and responding with empathy. What hasn't changed in the last 40 years is the end result. Patients, like all people, respond best when they feel respected and valued by those with whom they interact.

Doesn't all this sound great? Is it realistic in today's reimbursement-driven OT service delivery system? Do we have the time? "Well," said Red Jacket (to one who complained he had not enough time), "I suppose you have all there is." *Society and Solitude. Works and Days* Red Jacket's response is harsh but clear. We cannot just create more time. However, we can use the time we are allotted in the most effective way possible, and always remaining cognizant of the fact that time spent building relationships pays big dividends.

Building a bridge requires some time, but it mainly requires significant interpersonal skills. It is not just being friendly and supportive. Spend time learning and honing these skills and you will be surprised at how quickly a bridge can be built.

4. Advice = 'Add-Vice'

Because occupational therapists tend to be helpful and caring people, many of us are too quick to give advice to our patients, students, family members, and friends when they disclose their personal problems to us. A better approach would be to wait, listen and ask pointed questions. This allows people time to come up with their own solutions, and also shows that you are genuinely interested in trying to understand their situation. Giving advice is of course faster and easier than trying to pose questions that promote insight. But, as true change agents, we want people to be able to solve their own problems; not simply tell them what they should do or not do.

Recently, I worked with an 88-year-old patient in a Florida rehab program who was still adjusting to the death of her husband one year earlier. She was in occupational therapy after receiving a knee replacement. During treatment, she talked about being a snowbird, or one who flies south before the snow flies, and then back north in the spring. Her primary residence was in Chicago but she commuted to Florida each winter. However, maintaining two residences had become a burden since her husband's death.

I was working with her on dynamic standing during kitchen activities when she suddenly began to cry. I sat her down, gave her some tissues, and said to her: "Are you OK? What's going on?" She spoke of her two residences and wondered how long she could keep them both. We were in a small OT room that was occupied by two other patients and two other therapists—all of whom knew each other. It was not uncommon for everyone to join in any one else's conversation.

I asked the woman what part of her situation she found the most troubling. This is a technique I frequently use with people who are struggling emotionally. It helps them to focus their thinking and guides our conversation. Before she could respond, one of the other therapists jumped in with a solution: "Why don't you do what my grandma did and close up your Chicago apartment, and live down here full-time?" The patient didn't say anything, just continued to cry quietly. The same OT then said: "Oh, don't cry. Your knee is doing great and you will be discharged back to your house here that you love so much. You will see. Once you get home everything will look so much better. You won't be sad then."

The patient stopped crying and said, "Yeah, I guess." I then got her back to the kitchen activities preparing her for discharge.

So, was this patient's problem solved because she stopped crying and got back to her therapy? Of course not, and I found this out when I took her back to her room to work on ADLs. While working on donning and doffing shoes and socks she said: "I was thinking about what you asked me in the kitchen, and I think the part I find most troubling is that I want to start paying people to do the things I just don't feel like doing any more, but I'm being criticized for it."

I said, "It seems like you have thought this all out, and found a solution that works for you. So, what are the criticisms you are hearing?" This caused her to talk in detail about family members who said, among other things, that she is "getting lazy in her old age." She found these comments hurtful. She had always taken pride in being a hard worker and cared for her husband for three years prior to his death without any help. I believe my technique of gently probing moved her toward her own solution-finding (Remember, I'm a change agent!). It was rewarding to see her become energized about paying people to do things, and being resolute that "this is my business; not theirs."

Giving superficial advice is easy, but often not effective. In fact, I believe the tendency to give advice is a vice all its own. Think of advice as *add vice*. Because this is such a strong habit, it is almost addictive. It seems natural to try to quickly resolve a problem the moment we hear the gist of it, many times with inadequate or misinformation.

As OTs we can't help but want to fix everybody and we believe we often have the best answer or solution. We all have this habit of listening just enough to get the basic idea of the problem and then jumping right into solution finding. But, we often don't have enough information about the problem, or do not give the other person the opportunity to figure it out for him or herself.

Most people know more about their current situation and available resources than we do, so our advice may not be valued at times because to them it is not relevant. So, a true change agent does not fix people's problems; but instead helps people develop new perspectives on their problems and then they fix them themselves.

5. Proposing the preposterous

"Free yourself from the rigid conduct of tradition and open yourself to the new forms of probability."
Hans Bender (1907-1991) German Lecturer

I have discovered an unusual way of helping people to change that you won't find in any OT textbook. However, this strategy carries a risk with it. If not done in a timely way and very carefully, it can result in confusion and even alienation on the part of the other person. It is subtle and quite effective when applied properly with sensitivity by a skilled change agent.

I call this strategy *proposing the preposterous* and I have used it for years with patients, students, friends and family. It works best with a person who stubbornly clings to an unrealistic view of a situation or themselves. They may be caught up in what cognitive behaviorists call catastrophic thinking. They believe firmly that they are going to fail a course, lose their job, be sued, die, lose a loved one, get cancer, and so forth. This is the tunnel vision often seen in adolescents, but all people throughout the lifespan can experience this same narrow view of their world at times. I must point out that these people are not psychotic and in general have intact cognition. They just have a distorted view of their reality. Proposing the preposterous is what I use to help the person quickly move forward. Below are two examples.

I was treating a 61-year-old retired nurse for De Quervain's disease, which is inflammation of the tendons of the thumb. The nurse was a pleasant person with a great sense of humor, but she was terrified of getting Alzheimer's—the same disease that had caused her mother to "slowly rot away." She has had numerous tests in the past year and none of them suggested that she was developing Alzheimer's. Regardless, she would become very annoyed if she forgot anything or had trouble recalling someone's name. No amount of reassurance helped her. She viewed her occasional forgetfulness as a sure indication that she had the beginnings of the disease she dreaded so much.

Now a caution for overzealous change agents who are eager to help: If you begin *proposing the preposterous* too soon, the person thinks you are being intolerant, insensitive, or worse. Here is a better way that helped this nurse: After I validated her feelings on numerous occasions and supported and encouraged her over several weeks, I felt I had built up enough trust to make what may on the surface seem to be an outrageous suggestion. "Have you visited some of the Alzheimer's care units around the area to assess which would be a place you could be comfortable in?" She was taken aback, and asked in a low voice: "Do you think I should?" I said, "Well, you certainly seem convinced that you have Alzheimer's in spite of what the doctors have said, so, I guess the next step would seem for you to begin exploring and assessing different environments to find the best fit for you. Your background as a professional nurse would seem to give you a unique perspective on these different settings". She was at first very quiet and then she said, "Maybe I'll wait a bit because I am probably just getting rusty." From that time forward she seldom spoke of that old certainty that she had Alzheimer's disease, but when she did I always returned to my preposterous proposal.

A second example occurred in a non-clinical environment. I served as the academic advisor for a particularly anxious student. She was constantly fearful of failing a course or having her GPA fall below the minimal level and thus be dismissed from the OT major. She was a strong student who never received an academic warning, let alone come close to failing a course. I worked with this student for three years and had her in three of my OT courses, and felt confident in our level of rapport.

During one of her worst self-described melt downs, I said, "You know I have been thinking about you a lot lately and feel so bad for you. I have been investigating other majors for you and it seems social work would be far less stressful for you. I have the change-in-major form here, which I have already signed. All you have to do is fill it out, put the date next to my signature, and follow the routing instructions on the back. I think you would make a fine OT, but at what price?" She, of course, was shocked and became uncommonly quiet. Then she said, "Thank you for saying I would be a good OT. I think I over think and overreact to things. I don't think I need this form. I'm ok." I think *proposing the preposterous* within the context of a strong relationship has the effect of catapulting the person into a place where they can recognize their disparaging thoughts as being unfounded and sometimes even ridiculous. This technique gives them a higher level of insight that could never be reached by just giving encouraging words, or ordering them to "just stop talking so crazy." Yes, this is an unusual method for a change agent to work, but highly effective if done skillfully.

6. A 2x4 in the face

"Insanity is doing the same thing, over and over again, but expecting different results." Albert Einstein (1879-1955)
German-born theoretical physicist

There are times when our usual patient education methods just do not work. This is seen in people who tenaciously maintain a pattern of behavior that is rigid and a closed view as to their responsibility for the problems in their lives. It is these situations that often cause us to become frustrated and view the patient as unmotivated. We cannot seem to get their attention, and our change agent work does not work if the other person is not engaged. Of course, this behavior is not limited to our patients. It can be seen in our friends, family members, colleagues, and even ourselves. These situations require what I call the *2x4 in the face* approach. I offer an example below that illustrates how I used it with a particularly challenging patient.

A few months ago I was working in a hand therapy clinic with a 43-year-old woman diagnosed with bilateral carpal tunnel syndrome. She was a challenge in a number of ways. As a self-employed bookkeeper she did a lot of computer work, which, over time, contributed to her condition. But, being self-employed prevented her from qualifying for Workers' Compensation benefits. As a result, she was injured and without her income or insurance. Understandably, she was much stressed.

Her surgeon had performed a procedure called an endoscopic surgical release on her right wrist, which was her dominant hand, but she continued to have pain and weakness for weeks after. While in therapy, she called her surgery "a butcher job" and talked loudly about suing the surgeon.

In therapy, I was able to reduce her pain using Fluidotherapy and maintain her range of motion. But her hand muscles remained weak and exercises to strengthen them brought back severe pain. In spite of our best efforts, she did not make much progress. But, surprisingly, she continued to regularly attend therapy and, in fact, spoke very highly of our OT services.

During our time together, I got to know her well enough to realize that her Type II diabetes was not well controlled. She was overweight, disregarded nutrition guidelines, did not exercise and smoked a pack of cigarettes a day—all of which can obviously greatly impact her health, especially in her ability to recover from her condition (Carpal Tunnel Syndrome) and subsequent surgery.

One session, when she was once again complaining about her "botched" surgery, I spoke to her honestly and directly. When the other therapists were out of earshot, I said, "I was thinking about you and your surgery and thinking that maybe the reason that you did not get better results was because you smoke." She stopped talking for about 20 seconds—a rarity—and then said, "What do you mean?" I went on to explain in lay person's terms about the adverse effects of nicotine on tissue repair and healing. She listened closely and then became a little tearful as she described her past attempts to stop smoking.

We talked openly about smoking-cessation programs, the risks of diabetes, and her feelings of hopelessness and tendency to blame others. Our relationship changed because we both knew that she could no longer (at least with me) just complain about her condition without recognizing her contributions to her own impaired health.

I wouldn't have said this unless I had built a strong foundation of trust. Still, I recognize that sometimes this can feel like being hit with an emotional *2 x 4 in the face.*

I made no judgment of her. Nor did I attempt to solve her problems; just continued to ask questions that led to her accepting more responsibility for her health in general. I found it much more enjoyable to work with her as she began to make small changes in her life, and become more proactive regarding her poor health.

As OTs we need to be alert to these opportunities to confront our patients with reality, but only after a strong relationship of trust and caring has been established. Confrontation, or a *2x4 in the face*, without the foundation of trust can lead to alienation, non-compliance, and the patient's rejection of the therapist as well as OT. Trust with timely confrontation can lead to change, and that is what change agents do.

7. Just in case

"Prediction is very difficult, especially if it's about the future."
Niels Bohr (1885-1962)
Danish 1922 Winner of the Nobel Medal for Physics and
Chemistry

I met Jason in the 1970s in the Spinal Cord Unit of a large medical center. Jason, 17, had been in a car accident that severed his spinal cord at C-7, and left his legs paralyzed and he had only partial use of his arms and hands.

Due to the overwhelming depression that often accompanies such an accident, he was angry and uncooperative most of the time. During therapy, he proved difficult to work with, refused to use adapted equipment or participate in conversations about the best type of wheelchair and accessories he preferred. This stemmed from his deep religious belief that God would heal him. His parents also felt that their prayers and those of his church would restore him. Therefore, Jason thought it was "stupid" to talk about wheelchairs when he was going to walk out the door someday.

Unfortunately, Jason's refusal to participate in therapy led to a worsening of his condition. He developed a stage-3 pressure ulcer or bed sore on his lower back, had frequent urinary tract infections, and was losing range of motion in his shoulders, elbows, and wrists. Because he refused to attend occupational or physical therapy, the strength in the arm muscles that he could still use were also declining along with his endurance.

Because of his pressure ulcer, the nursing staff wanted him to spend more time in the prone position on his stomach to promote healing, but he would not comply. With him in mind I came upon a design for an adapted hospital gurney (stretcher on wheels) that Jason could perhaps propel himself from the prone position using the large front wheels. Again, he showed resistance, saying that "once I start walking my bed sore will heal right up."

I then decided to try a different approach, and said: "Let's go with the idea of an adapted gurney for you. I'll do all the work and get it working for you because it's so important to get you off your back just in case your ability to walk doesn't happen as quickly as all of us want". Those three little words, *just in case*, worked, and Jason began participating in his rehabilitation to a far greater extent. As long as everything we did with him in OT was preceded by the phrase *just in case* he did his exercises, tried adapted equipment, and reviewed the various options available for his motorized wheelchair we were getting ready to order.

Ever since, I have used this approach whenever a patient hangs onto a belief that they are going to get better when science says they are not. Denial, in this sense, can be a good thing. It gives people facing major losses the time to adjust. However, if patients take too much time to accept their new reality, they can lose even more function.

Therapists have to find the right balance between pushing the patient and giving the patient time. If pushed too hard, patients may become even more resolute or simply shut down.

I have found that balance works best. I try to maintain a sense of hope while offering a *just-in-case* scenario. It helps patients participate in therapy and accept help from others without feeling diminished. As they begin to participate in therapy, they not only improve their physical and emotional health, but also continue to work toward acceptance of the inevitable.

This approach is sort of a delayed way of doing change agent work. The patient isn't really changing their belief system, but they are changing their behavior. As time goes on they may cling forever with their *just in case* belief system, or they may come to the realization that their previous thinking was inaccurate. When this realization occurs, the OT as well as the rest of the staff and family must be ready and willing to provide an exceptional amount of support to help them through it.

8. To push or not to push

Few things in the world are more powerful than a positive
push. A smile. A word of optimism and hope. A 'you can do it'
when things are tough."
Richard M. Devois (1926-)
American Businessman and owner of the Orlando Magic,
NBA basketball team.

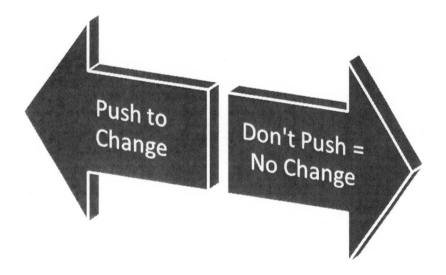

Figure 8-1. The "Push" or "Not Push" issue for OT practitioners.

While recently practicing in a Florida rehabilitation center, I was scheduled to see a 94-year-old patient who was hospitalized for general reconditioning. I went to his room and found him in bed, covered up, glasses off, and teeth out and sound asleep. He looked so peaceful and comfortable that I hated to disturb him, but I have a job to do. After calling his name and gently shaking him, he finally opened his eyes. I explained it was time for therapy. He responded by treating me as if I were a door-to-door vacuum cleaner salesman.

Politely but firmly, he said, "I have worked in college administration all of my professional life, and have held several high-level academic posts with great distinction. I no longer require or need any therapy. I just want to rest until it is my time to go."

He convinced me. I took his teeth and glasses and put them away, covered him back up and told my boss of my decision to let him sleep. She was pretty annoyed with me and said, "You have to get your productivity up," referring to Medicare reimbursement. "You have to go back and force him to get up for OT. If we don't get him moving he won't be able to go home to his apartment."

On my way back to his room, this same patient certainly shocked me by coming up the hall. He was propelling his wheelchair with his feet and had an enthusiastic look on his face. He didn't remember my visit a short time before so I reintroduced myself. This time he was happy to take part in therapy and off we went. He worked for 45 minutes on strengthening, endurance, and standing activities without complaint. What a different impression he gave from the one I experienced earlier that day. I wondered what happened.

This man personified one of my career-long struggles—when to push, or not to push, patients. When patients are medically stable, I have no problem pushing them. In fact, I felt a crazy pride when a patient once told me, "You know, you're a pain in the ass—a therapeutic pain in the ass, but still a pain in the ass." I loved her words so much I adopted it into my clinical reasoning teaching and began encouraging my students to each become a *TPIA* (Therapeutic Pain In the Ass) themselves.

But when patients seemed too medically ill, too depressed or too debilitated, I am reluctant to push. Sometimes, however, being a softie has gotten me into trouble. Imagine my shock when the patient I saw at 10 a.m. and decided was not capable of participating in OT was cheerfully taking part in physical therapy later that day. What did I miss? Should I have ignored the patient's complaints and pushed them?

Sometimes it seems that pushing is best for most rehab situations. Today there is even more pressure to push patients regardless of their condition because of reimbursement mandates. Medicare and other third party payers expect therapists to push patients through the rehabilitation process. However, I am also very aware of my responsibility to adhere to the OT Code of Ethics and to *do no harm*. I always want to help people, and certainly not harm them.

Sometimes the therapist has to not take no for an answer, for the good of the patient. But I have also had numerous experiences when patients were better off not being pushed. I, as well as other OTs, PTs and nurses have pushed patients only to discover later that they were suffering from cancer or other medical conditions that were the basis for their refusal. Some patients have died the day after a strenuous therapy session. Depression is different. People who are depressed need to be active and the "no-nonsense, just do it" approach (with support and encouragement) is exactly what they need.

What is obviously wrong is to push everyone regardless of their condition because of reimbursement mandates. What is equally wrong is to be too soft and easy on people. Always feeling conflicted about whether to push or not push patients is a good thing. When in doubt, seek the opinion of nurses who often understand who is capable of therapy and who should be allowed to rest. The nurses save me every time, and I think we should value and use the judgment of nurses more frequently than we do in these situations.

9. Overcoming OT Rejection

". . . I want to know if you can live with failure
yours and mine
and still stand at the edge of the lake
and shout to the silver of the full moon,
"Yes." . . ." The Invitation
Oriah Mountain Dreamer
Canadian story-teller and author

Every occupational therapist will experience clients who reject OT as a profession and at times the therapist themselves. These are not easy times—especially for new graduates. How can we begin to be change agents if the patient does not want us?

I experienced this in my second year of practice. I was working in a large skilled nursing facility that housed 640 patients, including more than a dozen patients under the age of 20. One of these younger patients was 15 years old when I first met him. Three years prior, his older brother had accidently shot him with their father's gun. As a result, he sustained a C-7 spinal cord injury, and thus had minimal use of his arms and no use of his legs. After he was medically and surgically stabilized, he was transferred to the facility for rehabilitation where I first met him.

He lived in a four-bed unit with three other young guys, and it was in this room where I experienced rejection. Around 10 a.m. one day, I went to their room to assess one of his roommates and found chaos. The nursing staff was trying to get all four of these total-care patients out of bed—a multi-step process that involved being washed, having suppositories inserted, having bowel movements, catheters inserted, leg bags drained, being dressed, and mechanically transferred to motorized wheelchairs. All four of the young men were swearing at the nurses, refusing to cooperate in any way and essentially having tantrums.

Within this stressful situation I introduced myself and attempted to help but was met with the same hostility. The young men had all experienced OT during their acute hospital stay and were not impressed. "OT sucks," they said, and they "didn't need or want any

32

OT." I said something lame like, "well, if you change your mind just let the nurses know," and left. This was OT rejection times four! No opportunity to be a change agent here!

I had plenty of other work responsibilities to worry about. However, the sting of rejection lingered. It was puzzling because, in the subsequent weeks, all four of these guys were quite friendly toward me, and often came to visit in their motorized wheelchairs when I was working with other patients. It was during these informal interactions that I got to know each of them and was finally able to build a bridge of sorts.

Then one day I realized what had happened on that awful morning when I first met them. I saw them in their most vulnerable states. They were undressed, being cared for by staff, not given any choices and talked to as if they were kids. They could not be the cool males they wanted to be. They were little boys in every way. This is what they saw me seeing and they couldn't take it. They had to drive me away in order to preserve their fragile and emerging male egos. So, when I viewed it like this I didn't feel so bad.

Informally, I began to work with the 15-year-old who had been shot on the problems he was encountering in his new life. For example, he loved to read paperback science fiction novels but he couldn't keep these books open with his lack of hand function. He had enough elbow and shoulder motion to turn pages in a magazine using a cock-up wrist splint and universal cuff with an eraser-pencil in it. However, this system did not work with paperbacks, which simply snapped shut.

So, he and I engaged in problem solving and came up with an idea to use a band saw (which we had access to in the maintenance shop) to cut off the binding of the book, and then drill holes through the paperback's edge to accommodate large key rings. We had a good laugh when we discovered that if we cut before we drilled, the pages went askew. Once we got the process down, he brought each of his new books to me and I set them up for him in this way. He was thus able to read his paperbacks independently.

He was very bright. In time, he earned his GED and began taking courses at a local college. I adapted a tape recorder and made him a new lap tray to accommodate his books and school supplies. Our relationship grew stronger with each problem we solved together.

Subsequent to my leaving this position, he formed a very strong relationship with one of the nurse's aides. Through the good work of his social worker he was able to be discharged to the community with the nurse's aide as his caretaker. They eventually married and were still doing well when I last saw them a few years ago at the funeral of the social worker that facilitated his discharge.

After three years in Syracuse I returned to Buffalo and had an opportunity to connect with this same patient, but in a different capacity. As part of a federal grant I received I needed to hire a grants-manager and thought he might be good for it. I contacted him, he loved the idea of using his business degree, and I hired him. He ran the grant for its one-year duration and did a good job. Who would have thought this all would have happened after he rejected me and OT several years prior.

From this and similar episodes of rejection, I learned to look beyond the surface when patients reject OT. Once, the underlying factors are known, it is not difficult to plan an effective way to respond. This approach is also good for our fragile OT egos. My role as a change agent got a slow start, but once underway I was able to help people who initially rejected OT. There is nothing like a different perspective to get re-energized about a problem that was once viewed as unchangeable.

10. "Seek first to understand . . . . "

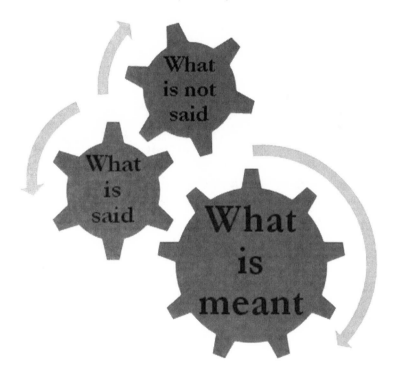

Figure 10-1. Results increase significantly when the focus is on understanding and not on being understood.

It is good to be an effective communicator in all things, but having the skills of a true active listener is essential as a change agent. Listening is the real building block in a relationship, and active listening is the mortar that provides the stability during difficult times. Our natural tendency is to focus more on ourselves than we do other people.

As a challenge, try having a five minute conversation with someone without using these words: *I, me, my, or mine.* If you are successful, you may already possess Habit 5 of the late Stephen Covey's *The 7 Habits of Highly Effective People.* This book, which is in its second edition, is an excellent treatise on personal growth and change. Dr. Covey had amazing insights into human behavior and wrote in a very engaging way. I had always assumed with this expertise that he was a clinical psychologist, but recently learned that he had a bachelor's degree in business, an MBA from Harvard, and a doctorate in religious education from Brigham Young University. He has written extensively and I think all OTs can benefit from his publications.

I like all of his seven habits, but especially number five: Seek *first to understand, then to be understood.* It may be the most challenging one to adopt because our habit in communication is the opposite. We tend to work very hard to first be understood. ("I tell them, and tell them, and tell them, and they still don't get it.")

This happens when healthcare professionals talk to their patients, when parents talk to their kids, when spouses and partners talk to each other, when supervisors talk to their subordinates, when teachers talk to students, when friends talk to friends, and so on.

It is quite commonplace, but few people see it as problematic as I do. When there is miscommunication it is not because someone didn't listen; it is because someone didn't ask enough questions and then listen carefully to the answers. Patient education is an easy place to see this deficiency. Consider a patient education session that starts with the OT explaining how the patient's peripheral neuropathy and carpal tunnel syndrome are due to the microvascular disease aspect of their diabetes, thus making self-stretching so important to their condition. The first time this is explained there is a lot of *telling and selling* and on the fourth time when the patient says, "I still don't know why I got carpal tunnel syndrome because I seldom use a computer" the OT may shift to *yelling.* A better way is to start by asking: "What do you know about the connection between your diabetes and your carpal tunnel syndrome"? The answer may surprise you, but their response will help you to know exactly where to direct your patient education.

Whenever you ask a really good open-ended question like this, actively listen as the patient answers, and paraphrase their words, the yield will be great. First, you will be showing great respect for the patient and their view of their disease. This forges a sense of trust and rapport. Perhaps more importantly, it reveals the level of knowledge your patient possesses. You will know exactly where the gaps and misunderstandings are, and thus will avoid boring or overwhelming the patient as you then go through your information (*seeking to be understood*). It also provides an opportunity to praise a patient's perseverance to learn about their disease, or to be empathetic about their efforts to carry on without correct information.

I have watched for people who have mastered this habit and tried to copy them. These are the people who ask you about your life and are really interested in your answer. They *don't* say: "How was your vacation because I canoed and camped through the Florida Everglades with my brother Sam's sister-in-law's neighbor's son Billy and his friend Al from Portland Maine, not Portland Oregon, where I first thought he was from, when Al asked if he could come with us. We saw, of all things, the biggest rats I ever saw. I expected to see alligators and snakes, which I saw a lot of, but I was shocked to see all the rats. Do rats eat fish? How do they catch them? Anyway, we had a great time and I learned that I can keep up with young boys and that they learned that a woman can do as well in the outdoors as men. I gotta go. See you. It was great talking to you."

I often think that there really are no difficult people, and this is such an important perspective when engaging in the change agent process. What I see instead are patients, students, colleagues, friends, and family who get into situations because they did not seek to understand and spent too much time and energy trying to be understood. When I had my private practice and had about 30 therapists working for me in a wide range of settings I was always either impressed or depressed when I would cover for different therapists. Because I wanted to know how much the new patients understood why they were receiving OT I would always ask: "How do you like OT?" or "What are you hoping to get out of OT?"

The answers were always informative. I learned that some hated OT, but loved the therapist or the socialization with other patients. Some came to OT because they thought it might help them. This information helped me to be more effective with each person. Depending upon the answer I could probe to understand their aspirations, fears, doubts, concerns, and level of understanding. Doing this in a conversational way while also providing treatment helped me to build a bridge with each patient without taking away treatment time. Once I understood, I could work on helping the patients understand how they could benefit from OT. This often changed a difficult patient into a motivated one, and I was doing change agent work.

Seeking first to understand, then to be understood can save so much time, confusion, and frustration in clinics, classrooms, homes, workplaces, and the community. We cannot really be client-centered and change agents if we don't ask the right questions and listen closely to the answers. However, doing this in a way so that the person does not feel interrogated is extremely important, and takes real skill.

Once I learned that some patients did not value OT, I realized that I actually had two problems. The immediate problem was the patient's knowledge gap and the other problem was that my therapists may have neglected Covey's Habit 5. I began seeking to understand the patients right then and there. Then, I had to educate my therapists and help them develop this important habit, which is a much longer process, but one that is well worth the time and effort.

11. This happened to the both of you

"Shared joy is a double joy; shared sorrow is half a sorrow."
Swedish Proverb

The first role of the therapist is to assess the patient and make a judgment about their level of cognition, physical capacities, and psychosocial functioning. But next, the therapist seeks to assess the family dynamics that may impact the patient's life.

Often when working with a new patient, I address his or her partner or caregiver at the same time if they are present and say things like, "This happened to both of you. Together you are both working to adjust to a lot of changes." It is a way of validating their emotions, building a relationship and letting each know that this was a journey they were both on. While a husband may have sustained a stroke and lost use of his right side, for example, his wife may have lost her job and independence in becoming his primary caretaker. Or a child may face the classic role reversal by having to take care of a parent. Because roles contain the entrenched habits and routines of daily life, no one makes the related shifts easily or without anguish.

I recall a 66-year-old patient I had worked with in the home-care setting who had cervical spondylosis, a condition in which progressive erosion of the joints of the neck resulted in deformity, pain, and loss of function. Also, she suffered from rheumatoid arthritis. She was unable to walk, and because of the deformities in her hands, unable to propel her wheelchair. In many ways she had the level of disability of a person with a spinal-cord injury (weakness and paralysis) except she had full sensation and pain.

Having always been the family decision-maker she was struggling with her role as patient. During one treatment session in which I was helping her to increase independence in feeding, she began to cry and blurted out, "everything is just so damn hard now."

Adding to her grief was the considerable tension between her and her husband. There were frequent blow ups, accusations, insults and profanity. And it didn't seem to matter that I was present. I continued to focus on the things that she wanted to work on (eating, propelling her wheelchair short distances, and transferring to the toilet) all while being immersed in their daily strife.

I continued to relate to them as if they were a couple experiencing the same disability. Since he was also a skilled home repairman with good mechanical problem-solving skills, I included him in the process of adapting things for her. They were struggling financially (he retired early to take care of her), and thus could not afford the equipment that Medicare denied. She needed a suspension sling to support her upper extremity while eating, and he made the necessary bracket and bar in his shop. I was able to create a sling to support her arm, and it all worked.

Throughout this whole process I put her in the position of what I called "the quality control engineer." If it didn't work to her satisfaction, then her husband and I were responsible for getting it right. She loved being in this position and he became more respectful toward her. The fights lessened (at least when I was around), and I think it was an indicator that she was establishing a new and more satisfying role. It also suggested that they were relating to each other as partners rather than as adversaries.

After eight weeks of OT we had reached the point where I felt good about discharging her. Over the coming weeks and months I would stop by periodically to see how they were doing, and was pleased that they were continuing to view her disability as *their disability*. They also were continuing to work together to attack the problems that arose as she continued to decline further. This approach helped to decrease the stress and strain in their home and in their relationship, and undoubtedly improved the quality of life for both of them.

My change agent role became a bit more complex because of the dual nature of the condition I was dealing with: her disability and loss of role, and his trying to adjust to his wife in a different role. However, by recognizing early on that her disability was both of their problem I was able to effect change in both of them.

12. What's the worst thing about this for you?

". . . you fix what you can fix and let the rest go. If there aint nothing to be done about it it aint even a problem. It's just aggravation". No Country for Old Men
Cormac McCarthy (1933—)
American novelist and playwright

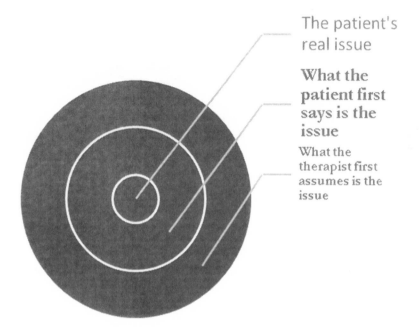

The patient's real issue

What the patient first says is the issue

What the therapist first assumes is the issue

12-1. Change begins when the patient states their true concern or issue.

When working in a busy rehabilitation center, I began assessing a patient who had sustained a severe stroke three months prior. The muscles on his dominant side were completely flaccid and he was unable to move them. Yet when I talked with this man about his goals for therapy, he said, "drive to Colorado"—very different goals than the ones I was already formulating for him in my mind, such as being able to eat with adaptive equipment and increasing the range of motion in his paralyzed arm.

It is not uncommon for people who acquire a disability to be overwhelmed and to be unrealistic about their therapy goals. As an OT and change agent I saw this as an opportunity to help him focus and prioritize his needs and wants. As therapists we see needs; patients see wants. The change agent process is to unify these different goals into ones that make sense and are desired by both the patient and the therapist.

Working in such fast-paced settings requires that therapists move quickly through assessments, including goal setting. It can be a frustrating experience when patients state unrealistic or even superficial goals, such as "get better," when therapists are trying to be client-centered while under a time crunch.

With my patient who wanted to drive to Colorado, I temporarily set aside the paperwork and asked a different question. I said, "Let's just stop for a minute and let me ask you something else. What is the worst thing about your stroke for you?" He paused for a minute, got tears in his eyes, looked away from me, picked up his paralyzed hand with his unaffected hand, waved it about, and said in a low tearful voice: "being a freak."

There it was. The driving to Colorado and range of motion conversation was completely irrelevant to his wants and my perceptions of his needs. His self-concept, self-esteem, and roles had changed dramatically causing him to feel worthless, unsightly, and ineffective. I almost missed this. I wondered how many other times I did miss it with other patients.

Now that I learned what this man was really experiencing, I told him that "in my experience strokes are one of the worst things that can happen to a person, but that life is not over; it is just going to be different." I then got him to pick one thing about his stroke that is most frustrating for him right now, and it was toileting. So, that became the short term goal and functional mobility the long term goal. He was able to hold off on the Colorado trip, and view his wheelchair and bed mobility along with transfers as mini-steps on the way.

I learned from this man to never make this mistake again. I now ask every patient regardless of the setting: "What is the worst thing about this for you?" If they cannot respond, I ask the patient's family members, caregivers, or friends. Also, I ask it in the beginning of the assessment so I help them get centered on their primary problem, and I don't get focused on the wrong things. It's the coalescing of needs and wants that is the basis for the work of a change agent. I believe this simple question is not only the essence of being client-centered; it also expedites the whole assessment and treatment-planning process.

13. When patients (think they) know best

"To know that we know what we know, and that we do not know what we do know, that is true knowledge."
Henry David Thoreau (1817-1862)
American Essayist, Poet, and Philosopher

It is always sad when I meet patients whose occupation is the pre-occupation with their condition. They spend hours on the Internet researching the latest treatments, downloading articles, and conferring with people with the same condition. This *occupation* can sometimes impede the process of change and adaptation because these patients may be consumed by erroneous information and suggestions. A big part of the change agent role is to respect the patient's perspective but through questioning and active listening also help the patient gain the perspective that will serve them best.

Recently, I experienced this very thing while treating a patient with complex regional pain syndrome (CRPS), a diagnosis that is confusing, contradictory and confounding. The chronic pain, loss of use of the hand, swelling, discoloration, and contractures associated with the condition pose major challenges to every aspect of one's life. The actual cause and treatment is confusing and fraught with contradictory opinions of experts.

Current research shows that a more conservative approach is the only way to temper this debilitating condition. However, this particular patient was questioning the validity of my therapy (in a pleasant way). My treatment consisted of contrast baths, constant active range of motion (AROM) and aerobic exercise. In contrast, her online support group was advising her that the only way to get better was to really stretch the muscles and joints of the hand aggressively, which research shows can actually worsen the condition.

She wasn't unique in today's culture. WebMD, Merck, Pub Med Health, Wikipedia, and so forth are readily accessible. Clients are becoming more sophisticated and ask some hard questions. I have been asked: "Wouldn't one of those weighted vests help my son concentrate more?" "Why did you make the splint with the wrist so flat?" "Why are the doctors doing tests on my wife's neck when all her pain is in her thumb?" These are all legitimate questions that we cannot ignore.

The best way to answer these questions is to be up on the evidence and not dismiss their efforts. I like to foster the climate where patients and their family members feel comfortable asking me these questions. I also encourage them to search, though this is problematic because patients may not fully understand what they are reading or evaluate the different levels of evidence. Because the searcher is proud of their search results they can become defensive when we challenge their sources or conclusions. The more diligent ones have large folders of studies they have downloaded, highlighted, and put numerous notes in the margins. These are truly educated consumers that we do not want to discourage or alienate by the way we respond when they bring it to our attention.

The first thing I do is commend their efforts. I tell them that it is great that they are taking the time to learn everything they can about their condition. I go on to explain that what they are doing is a part of our partnership. We are both searching for answers and ways to improve their condition. This is a form of validation of their efforts, but without validating their findings that may lack the highest levels of evidence.

I try to stop what I'm doing and give a quick scan at the information they have, and find something in it to genuinely praise. It may be simply saying that the person who wrote it seems to have a lot of experience with the condition. I also ask permission to make a copy of it so that I can read it more carefully later on. Yes, even if it's nonsense because to them it is scientific evidence ("it was on the Internet"), and I'm showing them respect by making the copy. Of course, when I do read it, I'm doing so with the lenses of an evidence-based practitioner. Most of the stuff patients bring to me cannot hold up to the rigors of scientific scrutiny, but it is important that we are careful in the way we tell them this. I always try to find something in the article that I can honestly say caused me to reflect and to re-examine what I thought was accurate information. I never outwardly praise evidence that is not accurate, nor totally discredit the nonsense. This keeps the relationship strong and serves as the foundation for education without alienation which is a very good change agent strategy.

The way I do it is to straightforwardly and clearly tell them why we can't get too excited about the findings or conclusions. The use of "we" is intentional to further reinforce the idea that we are in this together, and I frequently state this. This sometimes includes informing them (gently, but clearly) that the information they found does not relate to their condition. Getting autism confused with Asperger's is a good example with kids, and Guyon's tunnel with carpal tunnel happens with adults. I find that if I have built a firm bridge with the patient, they usually accept my point of view and discard their information. If it is early on in the "bridge-building" process, or if I am too direct in my criticism of the evidence they bring forth, they tenaciously hang on to the conclusions they have formed. This may lead to dissatisfaction or even non-compliance with therapy because we are "not doing what's stated right here in black and white." Maintaining a relationship of mutual respect and trust is always paramount with me.

Here's what I did with this particular patient with Complex Regional Pain Syndrome: I commended her for getting connected to the online support group, and reiterated what a difficult condition CRPS is for everyone but especially for the patient. These are statements of empathy and validation, but also reinforce the usual path this condition takes.

To avoid an "either or" choice (aggressive stretching or Active Range Of Motion) in this patient's therapy program I offered her additional information. Through my own searching I came upon a systematic review of CRPS that compared several excellent studies of CRPS. This was just published in 2011 in one of the most respected medical journals, and I knew it was sound science. Following the partnership relationship we had built over the past three months, I made a copy of the article for her and then reviewed the findings. It was a very sophisticated article, but I did my best to make it understandable to this very bright patient. It did not state the best outcomes of different forms of exercise, but explained why each person had to be approached on a case-by-case basis. In general, the article stated that the more aggressive the splinting and exercise, the poorer the patient did, but there were other converse studies.

She agreed that we needed to follow the best minds dealing with CRPS, and make adjustments for her specific responses. She was pleased to see how seriously I took her condition, and at the same time respected her as an individual.

So, we want to keep the information flowing from all sources, but provide the clarifications necessary to avoid decisions that do not serve our patients in the best way possible. Evidence-based practice takes on another dimension when the patient is at the center of the conversation, and makes for better OT. The role of evidence-based practice complements the change agent process and should be used whenever possible.

14. A Bridge over Troubled Waters

*"I was a little excited but mostly blorft. 'Blorft' is
an adjective I just made up that means 'Completely
overwhelmed but proceeding as if everything is fine and
reacting to the stress with the torpor of a possum. I have been
blorft every day for the past seven years."*
Tina Fey (1970—)
American comedian, actress, writer, and producer

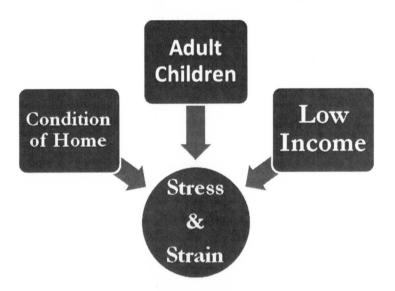

**Figure 14-1. The occupational stressors that impacts Clete's
health and sense of well-being.**

I met Clete ("That's all there is to my name, so take it or leave
it") in 1991 when I was doing home assessments for an agency
providing services to clients and their families with developmental
disabilities. Clete was the mother of a 28 year-old woman with
fairly severe cognitive deficits but who worked four days a week in a
supported employment setting. It was Clete's daughter Melissa that
the agency was working with to help her to eventually establish her
own apartment. The agency recognized that this goal was somewhat

unrealistic based on Melissa's needs, and that it would be better instead to add on to Clete's mobile home so that Melissa could receive the care she needed from her mother. The agency asked me to work with an architect to design a small apartment/addition attached to Clete's home so that Melissa could have her own life to a larger extent.

My assessment of Melissa also included assessing the home environment, and interviewing Melissa's mother Clete. This is what I saw when I met Clete, and these are the questions I had in my mind at the time: How does she endure this? What motivates her to carry on? These questions came from what I observed over three visits of assessment. Her three other adult children who lived at home and did not work did not put anything away or clean up after themselves. Her daughter Melissa had several developmental deficits and behavior problems that required ongoing care and support. Clete's car ran infrequently and when it did it seldom got her back home without something breaking down. Her double-wide mobile home was cluttered with many broken things that probably would never get fixed. Clete is overweight, has not been healthy for a long time, and cannot remember the last time she felt good. Without her teeth she refuses to attend church services that she always valued. Her relationship with her husband deteriorated many years ago, and he never comes around.

In spite of overwhelming problems surrounding Melissa the project was an interesting one and one that I looked forward to doing. However, Clete's life and home were really overwhelming for me. Clete loved Melissa and wanted the best for her, but she was burdened with so many things I wondered how she could survive all this. I explained all this in my report and presented it to the rest of the team when we gathered to discuss Melissa. I said there were three large obstacles preventing this from going forward: the condition of Clete's home; Melissa's need for support that was best provided by Clete; and Clete's maladaptive coping mechanisms. Therefore, the problem was one third architectural/financial, one third Melissa's developmental needs, and one third Clete's poor ability to manage the multiple stressors in her life. In a unique fashion, the team and the agency's administrator authorized the expansion of the project to address all three, and I was the one designated to help Clete cope along with the original intents of the project.

So, twice a week for six weeks I worked separately with Melissa, Clete, and the architect. Clete proved to be the most challenging and the most rewarding of my three spheres of intervention. The time with Clete was fascinating as she revealed her view of the world, that was equal parts fatalism ("That's the way God wants it. Don't mess with it") and unrealistic optimism ("When Melissa can drive I want to get her a nice car"). I had to help Clete face some hard realities, and take action in areas where she would normally be passive and accepting of whatever happens. Helping Clete become a proactive person was indeed a frustrating process for both of us, but it was definitely at the center of the change agent process. Because the "Problem List" for Melissa and Clete would probably fill several pages, I decided to focus my time with Clete on one thing: helping her manage her stress more effectively.

I started by having Clete work with me on creating her own personal "Bridge of Stressors". I explained how people are like bridges and that over time they wear out based on the stressors that are working on them. The key difference is that people, because of their minds, can do many things to decrease the negative impact of their stressors. Clete showed great emotion as she listed stressors like Melissa and her other adult kids, her "disgusting trailer", her weight, no working car, not enough money, and the constant arguing in her home. The real insight came from making a list of her stressors (she and I came up with 32), and then prioritized the list. I helped her pick some things to work on right now to get some momentum going and she chose to work on her eating habits (less fast food, stop snacking, eat more salads, etc.). The family had long ago stopped eating meals together, so her intended change in eating would not really impact others. She continued to prepare meals for Melissa and wanted to get her to also eat healthier, but knew that this would not be easy because as Clete said "that girl is a real snackaholic". I saw a different kind of thinking in Clete. She was not just accepting the latest crisis ("They just keep on coming.") she actually was slowing down her thinking and looking at alternatives.

The "Bridge Stressors" metaphor gave us a different way to talk about all the "stuff" going on around her. Sadly, she had little control over her adult kids who did not respect or listen to her. Not so sadly, in Clete's view, was that her second oldest son was arrested on burglary and assault charges, and was given two years in prison because this was his second related offense. Clete was actually relieved and said, "With him outahere I get his bedroom (she slept on the couch) and he can't be messing me up for a good while".

It was so good to hear her becoming assertive and proactive. The architect only did a fair job on the addition, and Clete was great about confronting her about the drawing's shortcomings. The agency had a federal grant that was going to fund the construction of the renovation of one part of the mobile home to give Melissa her own apartment with a connecting door. Everyone was pretty excited to see that this was really going to happen. I got to see it six months later when I stopped by. It was very nice, and Clete and Melissa found the separation from each other very therapeutic. Even though the rest of Clete's home was essentially the way I saw it on my first visit, Clete was a different person. She was coping better and seemed much happier. Hey, this change agent stuff really works.

Did Clete change in all the areas I had hoped? No, but I feel she acquired the insights to manage her stressors better. With these insights she could live longer, and have a better quality of life. Part of being a change agent is to always be in contact with reality, and not be living in "La LA Land."

15. From clumsy to competent

"I believe that we learn by practice. Whether it means to
learn to dance by practicing dancing or to learn to live by
practicing living, the principles are the same. In each, it is
the performance of a dedicated precise set of acts, physical
or intellectual, from which comes shape of achievement, a
sense of one's being, a satisfaction of spirit. One becomes,
in some area, an athlete of God. Practice means to perform,
over and over again in the face of all obstacles, some act
of vision, of faith, of desire. Practice is a means of inviting
the perfection desired."
Martha Graham (1894-1991)
American Dancer and Choreographer

Falls can be disastrous for older people, but just as disastrous
for younger people in a different way. Jamie, a fifteen year-old
young man with a myriad of developmental deficits, loved going to
McDonald's. The residential facility in which he lived was located
about a quarter of a mile from McDonald's, and the staff or his
father took him there at least twice per week. The problem arose
with the uneven surfaces Jamie had to traverse. If he stepped off
the sidewalk onto the gravel or misplaced his step up onto a higher
edge of the sidewalk, he would frequently fall. The falls resulted in
cuts and bruises, but when he broke his wrist things changed. His
father threatened to sue the facility, and the staff was chastised for
not providing Jamie with the necessary guidance and assistance.
McDonald's and other community excursions were thus eliminated
for Jamie's safety. Jamie was also restricted to the facility's grounds,
and could only go outside with a staff member present. Because
of staffing limitations Jamie could not go outside as frequently as
he wanted. He had been independent on the campus prior to this
ruling, and freely went from building to building. The autonomy
which he so much enjoyed had been essentially eliminated. What was
disastrous for Jamie were not the physical injuries from his frequent
falls, but it was his lack of freedom. This was a classic example of
occupational deprivation because community outings were his main

occupations. He had severe cognitive deficits that prevented him from understanding and adjusting to the rules that had now so restricted his life. His only way to react was with aggression.

I was asked to see Jamie because the staff found his aggressive behavior unmanageable. They knew this all started when his freedom was taken away, but they were under a mandate from Jamie's father and the facility's administrators to prevent him from falling. It seemed to me that the solution lied with Jamie developing the necessary mobility skills to manage uneven surfaces, and so I decided to create a program that the staff could carry out when I wasn't there. I felt that if Jamie could become more competent in walking and stop falling, he could get his life back.

My observations confirmed that Jamie had motor apraxia, a nervous system deficit that did not enable him to plan and execute movements of his body when the walking surface changed, nor could he quickly recover once he lost his balance. In OT, we have found that if we have people with apraxia learn how to navigate through an obstacle course, that this helps them to overcome this deficit. With this in mind, I created a simple obstacle course that required Jamie to go over and under low tables, through a tunnel, up and down stairs, and stand on one foot at various "stations". As much as possible I had him walk on exercise mats not only to protect him when he fell, but to also give him the sensory experience of uneven surfaces. He responded well to us going through the course together, and taking turns leading. The problem was his lack of patience. He thought the idea was to get through the course quickly, and he was not gaining the most from it regardless of the number of times he went through it. He was also very clumsy and knocked things over as he propelled himself on through with objects cast aside that were in his way.

I thus decided to add another element to the obstacle course in the form of bells as auditory cues. I found a bunch of one inch bells to which I attached strings. I then hung the bells all over the obstacle course at various levels and distances. I then explained to Jamie that we're going to go through the course without ringing any of the bells. At first he hit almost every bell, but I adjusted them so he could have some success. He got better and better at not ringing the bells, so of course, I had to change it up. I moved the bells closer together and changed the course itself, so he had to consciously pay attention to where his body was at all times. I also put different levels of exercise mats in his way so that when he fell (which he did a lot initially) he didn't get hurt. The staff continued this activity on a three times per day basis, and he became quite skilled at navigating the course without falling and without ringing any bells. We all enjoyed watching Jamie being so cautious and attempting to move gingerly over, around, under, and through the course. I also included music, and other people in the room that Jamie had to learn to ignore and concentrate on his movements. It was at this point that we took the obstacle course idea outside. We used the playground and the uneven surfaces around the facility as further training areas, and discontinued the bells. With just verbal cues to slow down and to look where he was going before placing his feet he become far more competent and less clumsy.

The final place to practice Jamie's new motor panning skills was in the swimming pool where I instructed staff on how to provide further challenges by gently pushing him from side to side and front to back as a sort of game. He liked the game and got very good at catching his balance when pushed off balance without warning.

At this point I did a re-evaluation of his motor planning skills and found him to be far more competent in this area. It was my recommendation that he be allowed the level of autonomy he previously enjoyed including a return to his beloved McDonald's. The staff agreed completely, but Jamie's Dad was skeptical. I met with him and convinced him to join us on a trip to McDonald's. He agreed, and on my next visit off we went to McDonald's. Jamie walked at a much slower pace, and watched carefully where he placed his feet. The trip went well, and Jamie's Dad changed his view of Jamie. So, the restrictions were lifted and Jamie had his life back. All from a bunch of bells strategically placed and graded in difficulty.

It is not uncommon for us as OTs to rely on caregivers and family members to carry out our intervention programs. Our expertise in activity analysis and in gradation of activity is often what is needed in order for people like Jamie to function at their highest level. Once we have this information we can train others to carry out a program like Jamie's, and see our change agent contributions come to fruition.

16. From 'whiner' to teacher

*"Inside of a ring or out, aint nothing wrong with going
down. It's staying down that's wrong."*
Muhammad Ali (1942—)
American former boxer, philanthropist, and social activist

At first, I was not enthusiastic about meeting Jim. The physical therapist asked me to see him because she found him to be a "whiner and a wimp." Jim was 56 and had been diagnosed with amyotrophic lateral sclerosis (ALS) or Lou Gehrig's disease six months prior. He was living in a skilled nursing facility when I first met him.

ALS is a progressive disease that destroys the motor neurons, ultimately paralyzing most muscles in the patient's body, including those that control vocalization, digestion and respiration. Knowing the poor prognosis of his condition in that people with it seldom lived for more than five years and his reputation for being difficult, I approached him with some trepidation. But, actually he was friendly, gracious, and very motivated. Physically, he reported having severe pain in his legs due to frequent muscle spasms. He had minimal use of his arms, but he did have intact sensation and cognition. When I asked him my favorite question: "What was the worst thing about this for you?" Jim said, "Being fed like a baby with everything mixed together." We agreed to work on the goal of eating independently, though Jim was not optimistic.

I shared my findings with the PT, who had forgotten that patients with ALS continue to experience sensation in their paralyzed muscles and had written off Jim's complaints of leg pain as "whining." She changed her attitude toward him immediately.

On my next visit I brought supplies donated by my previous home-care patients. I attached an overhead sling to the back of Jim's wheelchair to take advantage of his grade 2 strength in his deltoid, triceps, and brachioradialis. With his arm suspended and gravity eliminated he could now flex and extend his elbow in the horizontal plane, a position necessary for eating. His ALS left him with wrist drop so I made a cock-up splint to position his wrist at 30 degrees of extension so he wouldn't drag his hand through his food.

Jim had a great sense of humor and enjoyed observing and reacting to this whole trial and error process. His grasp was very weak except when his fingers were almost fully extended—preventing him from holding a spoon. I used sponge-tubing to build up the handle of the spoon, which he was then able to hold quite well. I stabilized his plate with a rubber mat, and put a metal guard on his plate so he could push food against it. This all worked great except he still could not bring the food to his mouth. Because he could only get the food to about where his Adam's apple was he laughed and said "just cut a hole in my throat and I'll be all set."

I realized that he lacked enough strength in his supinator muscle and could not rotate his forearm. As a solution, I tied about 10 rubber bands together, attached one end to the top of the overhead sling and the other to the proximal end of his spoon, and Bingo! The rubber bands provided just enough assistance to supinate his forearm so Jim was able to eat independently. He was thrilled and so was I. This was change agent work at its best!

I showed the nursing and dietary staff how to set up the equipment so Jim could eat independently. This enabled him to eat most meals by himself in his own way, which greatly improved his outlook. He asked me if he could eat a Big Mac by himself. His five adult children came to see him frequently and took him out to eat. He loved McDonald's but hated being fed especially in public. I rigged up a sandwich holder with a universal cuff and taught two of his adult sons how to set up the suspension sling apparatus. We practiced in the dining room until Jim could comfortably eat at McDonald's with his children.

As Jim's world expanded, he became concerned about the nursing home environment in which he lived. I encouraged him to run for president of the Resident Council. He won and became the spokesman for the residents and their advocate with administration. His ALS progressed and he had difficulty at times with speaking. But another resident who was elected secretary filled in the gaps. If residents found the food too cold, medications late, loud-speakers too loud, and so forth, Jim worked to solve the problem, even maintaining a sense of professionalism by wearing a tie during meetings or appointments with department heads.

It was during this whole trial and error process that I saw that a big part of Jim's role and occupation was socialization. He was very interested in people and seldom talked about himself. His way was to make everyone feel respected and valued regardless of who they were. He was a natural bridge builder of relationships which certainly helped sustain him in his daily struggles with his terrible disease.

His strength declined and again he needed assistance with eating. But he always tried as much as he could to do it by himself. Jim was a realist and knew his prognosis. He was also a spiritual person and viewed his disease as God's will. This perspective gave him a calm demeanor and positive outlook in spite of his grim prognosis.

Then one day John told me that he would like to teach again. He had been an art teacher in a grammar school before becoming ill. The activities director was resourceful and called the school where Jim used to work. After discussions with the principal, who had been a friend of Jim's, the second-grade teacher agreed to walk her class the two blocks from the school to the nursing home once per week.

The following Wednesday, the teacher and the activities director became Jim's voice and hands as he made suggestions to the children on their art projects. This happened every week for nearly two months, until winter weather prevented the children from trekking over. But for the time it lasted, Jim was once again an art teacher and he loved it.

Unfortunately, Jim's ALS moved into its final stages and he could no longer get out of bed. He could hardly speak and required feeding tubes and total nursing care. His mind was still clear and I always stopped to see him even though he was no longer on my caseload. I had to do all the talking by then but he enjoyed my visits.

My wife and I stopped there while on the way to the facility's holiday party. Jim enjoyed meeting my wife, who is very friendly and outgoing, and he remarked in a very laborious way that I had robbed the cradle. Then he laughed with a great deal of coughing and choking but smiling through it all.

The following week we left for a trip to Florida. Jim died while we were away. When we returned home we found a package sent on his behalf before his death. It contained a tie for me and a plant for my wife. Jim had asked the activities director to send it with a thank-you note. I make a point to always wear the tie whenever I lecture on ALS or tell his story to communicate what great things can come from OT that is client-centered and occupation-based.

17. A picture book for Sal

"We shouldn't teach great books; we should teach a love of reading."
B.F. Skinner (1904-1990)
American Behaviorist, Author, Inventor, And Social Philosopher

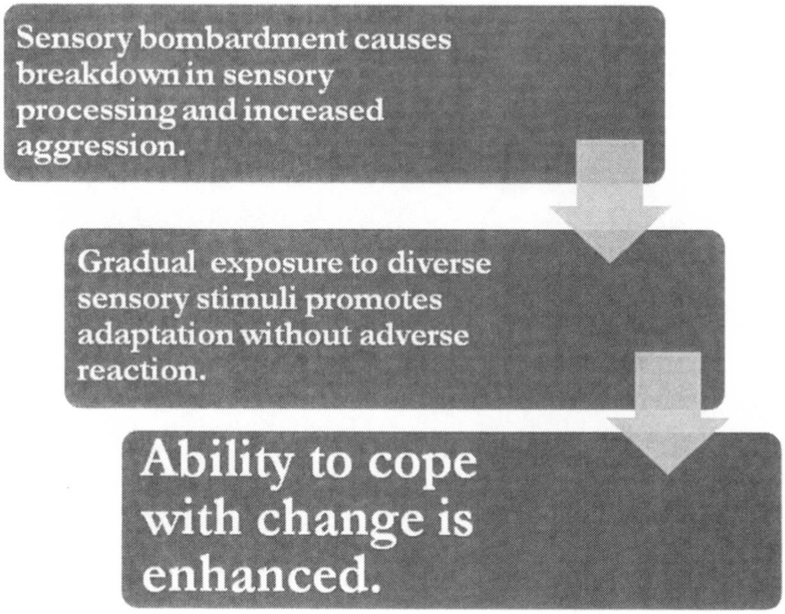

Sensory bombardment causes breakdown in sensory processing and increased aggression.

Gradual exposure to diverse sensory stimuli promotes adaptation without adverse reaction.

Ability to cope with change is enhanced.

Figure 17-1 Sal's ability to cope with change is directly related to the intensity and quantity of the sensory stimuli present in his immediate environment.

Imagine a large teenage boy who constantly screamed, punched himself, slammed his head into tables and pounded on the walls. I didn't have to imagine, for this was Sal—a 16-year-old with autism who was living in a residential treatment facility for children with severe developmental disabilities.

This treatment program was located in rural Pennsylvania where I provided consultation services on a weekly basis. The facility was made up of a few cottages that housed eight residents ranging in age from 10 to 21. All were medically stable, but behavior-management issues put a strain on the staff members, who frequently sought my advice. A clinical psychologist on staff was very helpful in designing behavior modification programs and training staff in their implementation. However, Sal was not responding to the system of rewards and the withholding of privileges, and so I was asked to see him.

I was a bit overwhelmed (actually a lot) when I first attempted to assess and interact with him. He was screaming and hitting himself while staff yelled at him to stop and counted hits with a mechanical clicker. On bad days, the clicks would reach 500. He would seldom strike others, and usually only did so when the staff tried to force him to stop hurting himself.

He was only quiet when staff got him to sit on the floor and look at two homemade picture books—three-ring binders with photocopies, one about grapes and the other about the circus. He seemed content to go through the books repeatedly while stating what each picture was. This would last for about 5 minutes and then he was up and back to punching himself and screaming. Sal did not possess a rich and diverse range of occupations, but those he did possess (grapes, circus, and I learned later on was his family) had significant ability to attract and engage him. The alternative of self-injurious behavior was certainly not the occupation that would be best for Sal. An alternative was needed.

At first, I tried diverting his attention with a beach ball or a stuffed animal, but he ignored them. As part of my assessment I met Sal's mother. His family lived within an hour of the facility and was very involved in his treatment program. He lived at home until two years prior when his size and behavior prevented his family from being able to care for him. She told me about a previous effort to help Sal that was disastrous from a number of perspectives.

What had happened was that the staff had tried capitalizing on Sal's interest in one of his books and took him to the circus as a reward for keeping his hits to less than 200. Sal's mom accompanied two staff and three other residents on the trip. But it turned out to be a one of the worst activities that they could have chosen. Sal's reaction to the circus is one that an OT could have predicted, but shocked the staff and Sal's mother. He had one his worst meltdowns when he went inside the large tent and saw three of the acts being performed at once. The loud music, bright colors, and all the people was too much sensory stimulation for Sal's sensory system. They had to immediately bring him back to the facility. Because their efforts to expand Sal's world were so disastrous, the staff and Sal's mom were very disheartened.

I recommended a different approach. Sal found safety and comfort in his books and his family, so I decided to use these to expand his world in a gentler way. I asked Sal's mom to take photographs of his family members doing things that were unusual and funny, but still familiar to Sal. For example, I had them take a photo of Sal's dad sitting in their dry bathtub with his clothes on; their dog standing on their kitchen table; his Mom using the lawn mower (which she never did); his sister working with tools; and so forth. I explained to Sal's mom and the staff that the idea was to gently and humorously prod Sal to explore the world beyond his rigid routine by pairing the familiar with the unusual.

We had the photographs enlarged on a copy machine. Then I inserted two of the 12 pictures randomly in Sal's circus and grape books. It worked! Sal would go through each book, and say the name for each object ("red grapes, clown", etc) in a rote kind of way with a look of real pleasure on his face. Then when he got to one of the unusual photos he would stop, study it closely, and say something like: "What is my dad doing in the bathtub with his clothes on?" A look of great joy appeared on his face as he looked at the new photos.

I instructed the staff to insert two more of the unusual photos into each book, and to also remove two of the routine photos over the next two weeks. I also cautioned them that if he reacted negatively to missing photos, they should re-insert them. His family loved the project, and began taking more and crazier pictures of people Sal knew doing unusual activities.

Sal began to hit himself less due in part to the new photos. The unusual photos quickly became so interesting to him, that we put them all in separate books. When given a choice Sal always chose what we called his family book instead of the grapes and circus books. In fact, I encouraged the staff to stop talking to Sal about the circus and grapes and to talk instead about what was going on in the pictures. When he went home for visits, he wanted his family members to reenact the various activities and was delighted when they did so.

The staff joked that I was a wizard, but it was OT common sense not wizardry. It was knowing how the nervous system can accommodate to changes in stimuli if the differences are not too great or intense. The live circus was certainly beyond Sal's ability to cope and adapt, but the gradual use of the unusual photos was the just-right challenge for him. We expanded Sal's occupational world and gave him a greater source of joy. The evidence was in the decreased hitting that staff and his family readily noted.

18.   A 'doer' even while dying

"Because I could not stop for Death,
He kindly stopped for me.
The Carriage held but just ourselves
And Immortality"
Emily Dickinson (1830-1886)
American Poet

When working for a home health agency that also provided hospice care, I was assigned a patient, "Sam," whom I quickly realized had the personality type of a real *doer*. She was energetic, organized, direct, and was intolerant of time being wasted by others and especially her.

Sam had worked as an assistant principal at a large high school when she developed breast cancer. For two years, medical interventions had kept Sam's cancer in check. Even while undergoing an exhausting treatment regimen, Sam worked full-time and took care of her husband and three children. She scheduled her double lumpectomies during school breaks. Even during chemotherapy, she limited the days she took off from work to rest.

In spite of the cancer, Sam made it clear she was the same person. Her co-workers, friends, husband and three teenage kids all knew that to treat her any differently would make her life, and theirs, miserable. With Sam, it seemed that difficult things like one's cancer should be dealt with as quickly as possible, and should disrupt other people's lives as little as possible.

Of course, I learned all this about Sam after working with her for a month and she is someone I will never forget. Being a change agent for someone who is dying is not any different than with anyone else. Their values, interests, and occupations still have the power to engage and influence life even as it is diminishing. That is probably the biggest difference in that time is limited, and is of course not far away from everyone's thoughts.

By the time I saw her, Sam's cancer had returned and quickly incapacitated her. After six weeks of aggressive treatment, doctors recommended hospice care. After reading her hospice chart in the office I was not expecting to see someone as vibrant as she was. After I introduced myself as an occupational therapist, she said, "I do not expect to be returning to work and I certainly do not have any developmental delays, so why did they send an OT to see me?"

I explained that there are different kinds of OT and the type of OT we do in hospice care is entirely driven by the patient. She then said, "So, if I say I don't think I need or want OT, you'll go away?" I said, "Yes, but not quickly or easily because I think we could work well together and that I can help you." Sam, looked at me closely, was silent for a moment, and then said, "OK, let's see what your kind of OT can do for me."

I then asked my favorite question, but in a different way, "What is the worst thing about your life *right now*?"

Sam, who was sitting up in bed, slammed her fists into the mattress with more energy than I expected, and with tears in her eyes said, "I'll tell you. It's waiting for incompetent people to do the simplest things, and then have to repeatedly remind them to either do it, or how to do it right." It turned out that she was talking about her husband, her sister, her kids, her minister, her home health aide, and just about anyone else that she had to now rely on. I felt I could easily be added to her list.

It has been my experience that people who have led independent lives find accepting help from others absolutely intolerable. They take pride in not being a burden on others. What seems to go along with this lifelong striving for independence are excellent time-management and organizational skills. Friends and relatives see them as the real doers, and this carries over to the world of work as well. These people are usually the stalwarts of families and companies. People depend on them and have come to expect them to effortlessly and quietly carry the greater load. Being thrust out of this role can be almost as difficult as the illness itself. Sam was struggling with this unwanted role that was thrust upon her.

People who always strive for excellence can be both a blessing and a challenge to OTs. I have worked with several people like this and know to look for the blessing in their motivation. They want to return to the life when they were the strong one in the group. However, no matter how motivated, there are times when the disability is just too great, such as with Sam. This is where the challenge comes in: getting them to accept help.

I said to Sam, "I can tell you have excellent time-management skills and you know the value of prioritization. So, what bothers you the most around here?" She said, "The bills and endless stream of mail that must be addressed."

I then asked, "What would it be like for you to teach one of your kids to take over this responsibility for now as well as for the future?" She was reluctant, believing they had enough to deal with. After some thought, she said, "Mark could do it, but he is working so hard to get a college scholarship that I would hate to take him away from that."

Then I turned to another tool in my tool kit: reciprocity. I have learned that people who do not like receiving help find it easier to make a deal. I asked, "Do you think reciprocity could work here? You do something for him that he dislikes and he in turn takes over the mail and the bills. What do think?"

She quickly said with a smile, "he does hate cutting the lawn and, actually, all outdoor work." She decided to get estimates from landscapers while appointing her son, the "bills and mail guy."

I was able to document my OT intervention plan under home-management skills. Over the next few weeks, I worked with Sam on other issues, including helping her accept the shower bench when she was determined to stand, though it was no longer safe. This time I used a metaphor, telling her that the captain of the ship (Sam) had to rely on the guy up in the crow's nest (me) to see a disaster ahead. This reframing made it easier for Sam to accept help. She also liked being viewed in this way.

Sometimes patients who adamantly refuse help are the ones who need it most of all. It is easy to become frustrated. But, if the therapist has respect for the patient's motivation, they can help keep them in their role of a doer, even while they are dying.

Everyone wants to remain engaged in their valued occupations as long as possible, and we as OTs can help by adapting the activity or the environment. Of course, a time is always reached in hospice care where the patient's condition precludes participation, and then the participation becomes more passive. Talking about and viewing pictures of better days and times can still be motivating and engaging for the patient. It also provides a meaningful role for family and friends who don't often know what to say or do when visiting. This is exactly what I did with Sam and her visitors right up until she died.

19. You never know

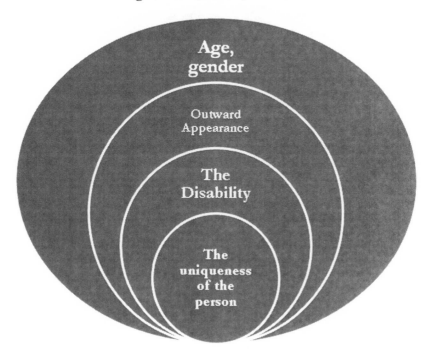

**Figure 19-1. The layers of a person can sometimes cause us to
miss the essence of the person.**

While working in a large skilled nursing facility, a nurse once
asked me to see a man whom she hoped I could help. She was fond
of him and wanted him "to get more out of life and not to just exist."
Initially, I was skeptical, thinking that the man was probably bored
and needed more from activities staff than from an occupational
therapist. But as a favor, I went to see him. Upon review of his chart,
I was further discouraged when I saw that he was 83 years old with
severe loss of function due to Parkinson's disease. Could a person

this debilitated benefit from OT? Wouldn't the change agent role be inappropriate with him? Could I employ the power of occupation, or would rest be his only occupation?

I went looking for him and found him sitting in his wheelchair in a corner of the Day Room. He was slumped down and seemed to be sleeping. I called his name but got no response. Then I shook him gently and he raised his head with a big smile.

Due to the muscle rigidity stemming from his disease, he was unable to move any of his extremities. His breathing was so poor that he could not vocalize beyond one-word responses, and these were laborious and usually unintelligible. He was so debilitated, I was not sure I could help him. But his smile and eyes were so engaging that I decided to put him on my caseload to see what I could do. However, I was not expecting much to come of it.

Our first goal of working on feeding proved unobtainable. So we moved on to work on increasing head and neck mobility. Because he was essentially non-verbal I had to rely on facial expressions and head nodding or shaking in response to my questions. Still, he was always able to communicate with his pleasant demeanor showing appreciation of any efforts to help him.

In an effort to compensate for his lack of arm function, I made him a head pointer with a rubber tip on the end of the stick. With a magazine attached to a vertical board clamped to a bed table, he was able to turn the pages and read. I then decided to broaden his activities and attached a paint brush to the end of his pointer. This enabled him to paint ceramic pieces that he donated to the gift shop. His level of excitement was evident every day when he was wheeled into the occupational therapy room. Apparently, coming to OT was the best part of his day.

Next we worked on communication. I was able to get an electric typewriter donated to the department for therapeutic purposes (they did not have computers in those days). Once I positioned the typewriter at just the right height, he used his head pointer to laboriously type out: "I am so happy. Thank you."

The ability to communicate quickly enhanced his world. He typed out questions for me, told me what he had been thinking about and shared his terror of choking to death. We met with a speech pathologist the next day, who showed him how the swallowing process worked and tested his gag reflex, which was intact. She was confident that he was safe from choking. Upon hearing this, he began to cry and typed out, "You are both angels. God sent you to me. Thank you."

A few days after this meeting he typed out another powerful message, "Can you find my wife? The last I heard she was living in a nursing home in Glens Falls, NY." This was a shock because we had no idea he even had a wife. I contacted his social worker, who researched it and was able to confirm the patient's wife was indeed living in a nursing home in Glens Falls. (This was about five hours from where he was living.)

With the couple's respective social workers acting as the mediators, the two were able to communicate through letters for the first time in years.

Our therapy sessions thus expanded yet again. Now he wished to be able to write letters to his wife. Every day he came to therapy to work on them. It was a painstaking task but he was diligent. His letters were about their past and his present life. He often brought a letter from his wife that I read to him. It was also filled with reminiscing but hers was more future-oriented. She wished to live out their final days together.

Within three weeks, the patient's excellent social worker was able to have his wife transferred to our facility. The nursing staff rearranged patients so that the couple could have a large room to themselves. Everyone regarded them as if they were newlyweds.

His life with his wife became his new valued occupation, and he enjoyed being a husband again. He no longer had time or the need for OT. I would often stop to see them, and they were always glad to see me. Little did we know that he would only have one year of life left. But the two were able to spend it together. Even as his physical health declined, his emotional health was much higher than that of the man I first saw sitting alone in a corner of the Day Room.

So, when you think nothing much can be accomplished by putting a much debilitated patient on OT, remember, you never know. The results show once again that engaging people in valued activities or occupations can have unexpected and great consequences.

20. Making the most of mistakes

"My heroes are the ones who survived doing it wrong, who made mistakes, but recovered from them"
Bono (Paul David Hewson) (1960—)
Irish Singer, Musician, and Humanitarian

While working in home care, I evaluated and treated a 58-year-old patient who had sustained a stroke six weeks prior. Overall, she had recovered well—at least physically. She had some lingering problems with her coordination and dexterity in her non-dominant hand, but walked fine and was moderately independent in taking care of herself. The larger problem was that the patient, Maureen, was showing problems with judgment, decision-making and impulsivity—personality traits that manifested with the condition, according to her daughter.

For example, Maureen had put packets of flower seeds in her freezer, mailed her credit card bill and payment to her church, became alarmed when she thought a hurricane in the southern states was happening to her town, which was 2,000 miles away, and told the paper boy to stop bringing her so much mail. She also neglected to hold a handrail when using stairs and had quite a bit of clutter throughout the house that could cause her to fall. To some, these may appear to be small things, but when taken together they showed that Maureen was at risk for injuries and being taken advantage of.

Being a change agent with patients with significant cognitive deficits can range from challenging to disastrous. Their ability to participate safely in their valued occupations can at times be quite risky. A gourmet cook, hot liquids, and deficits in decision making are usually bad combinations. So, in these instances, I employ a somewhat unusual strategy.

I decided the best approach was to let Maureen make mistakes. But let me explain: Sometimes protecting patients from failure is a disservice. Instead, I like to look for opportunities for patients to experience small failures as a form of feedback and learning.

This may sound unprofessional and uncaring, but it is just the opposite. I care very much about each patient, and I try my best to help them. There are times however, when my best efforts do not get the intended results.

After evaluating Maureen and talking with her daughter, I decided to have her OT program be directed toward safety and independence in self-care and home management. However, I made this plan with concerns about how successful it would be, and my concerns were validated after just three visits.

Each day was spent in giving Maureen cues to follow the correct sequence in each task (dressing, showering, grooming, meal preparation, dish washing, and so forth), but she repeatedly skipped steps. Also, her ability to recognize errors in her performance was minimal. It was not unusual for her to attempt stepping into the shower without checking the water temperature, or leaving food items in the microwave with beeping going on.

Her daughter was very frustrated with her and yelled frequently to try to get Maureen to pay attention. I was more matter-of-fact with a calmer voice and tried to get Maureen to think ahead or to reflect on her mistakes, but was not any more successful than her daughter. I knew a different approach was necessary.

In these situations where the verbal message is not grasped or retained, I use or even create scenarios where the patient experiences some adverse consequences but without being physically harmed. It seems a certain level of shock is necessary to help the patient to *get it*. I would let Maureen go a little further with a wrong decision as long as she was safe.

An example of this occurred when I stopped by to see her on a re-scheduled visit that she apparently forgot about. It was August; about 90 degrees out, and I found Maureen sitting on her porch with a winter coat and fleece hat on. She was waiting for a friend to pick her up to go to a church service.

Normally, I would have helped her change to fit the weather and avoid the embarrassment of having her friend see her dressed so inappropriately. However, I saw this as an excellent time to use her poor decisions as a learning opportunity. After asking her if she was too warm, she said, "No, I'm perfect, just toasty."

I then took her to look at the outside thermometer on the side of her house to see that it did indeed register 90 degrees. She looked at it and read it out loud at my request, but was not concerned at all.

As we were walking back to the front of the house, Maureen's friend pulled up. I gestured for her to park and join us on the porch. It was clear that her friend was in shock, and said sternly to Maureen, "Have you lost your mind? Do you know it's almost 100 degrees out (she exaggerated, but I let it go) and you're dressed like an Eskimo. I'm not going to take you anyplace dressed like that because I will look like a bigger fool than you."

Her delivery, facial expression, and emotional tone were perfect for my purposes. I let this harsh message sit for a few seconds, and then stepped in with a supportive message and asked Maureen, "What do you think about what she just said? She is right, you know."

With that, Maureen began to take off her coat and hat, and said, "I guess I should have checked the thermometer before I got dressed." This was the most insightful statement with recognition of an error that I ever heard from her. I gave her lots of praise for this, and off she went with her friend in a sleeveless top.

Why did Maureen respond to her friend with insight and compliance and neither her daughter nor I could get such a response? I think it was because of the emotion generated by her friend's unrestrained shock, and Maureen's desire to appear competent. I decided to use Maureen's future errors in the same way. I used the mirror a lot as the feedback mechanism to get her to self-assess the condition of her clothing, make up, and hair. She would often be somewhat embarrassed when I had her look closely at her appearance and she discovered a mistake like lipstick applied too broadly. To lessen her embarrassment, I would say something like, "It's no big deal. No one saw you but me, and I'm not telling anybody." This would make her laugh.

The kitchen gave me another arena for Maureen to practice discovering and correcting mistakes. At times it made a mess that she and I had to clean up, but the impact was worth it. I let the sink overflow when she left the water running, but I would never let any of her mistakes cause injury to herself or any damage to her possessions.

When I saw that she had neglected to do a next step correctly or neglected a step I would stop her and ask: "What will happen if you let this go in the microwave for the 20 minutes you set?"

Or, when making her breakfast I would ask before she ate them: "How did all those egg shells get in there? What can we use to get them out"? What would happen if you ate them? What would your friend think if you served this to her?" Of course my questions were never asked in this rapid-fire format because I wanted her to have time to reflect and learn.

All of my questions were intended to develop insight in Maureen and help her to become safe as well as independent. I never let my words or tone show annoyance, ridicule, or criticism. I just matter-of-factly asked my questions and got her to see her errors. There was also a lot of laughter as she discovered some of her errors and this helped her look at them in a more positive way.

I taught this approach to Maureen's daughter who welcomed a better way to help her mother. Both she and her daughter were able to look at Maureen's mistakes differently. Maureen had developed the insight to anticipate consequences, and to stop and check before proceeding. She also, on her own, put sticky notes around the house as prompts to include steps she usually neglected. Overall, Maureen did very well and at the end of a month I was comfortable in discharging her from OT.

Often, when people have severe cognitive deficits they lack the ability to learn new information or to transfer old learning to new situations. This makes being a change agent role more directed towards changing the environment rather than the patient. However, Maureen's deficits were such that she was able to learn and transfer learning to new situations. As a result she could remain engaged in far more of her valued occupations and have a higher quality of life.

21. Synchronizing the Men's Club

"Life is occupied in both perpetuating itself and in surpassing itself; if all it does is maintain itself, then living is only not dying."
Simone de Beauvoir (1908-1986)
French Existentialist Philosopher

In 1971, I took on a Saturday morning job as an activities program consultant in a small facility. Today it would be considered an assisted living facility. I was only out of OT school a few months when I decided to take on a new role. The experience was significant in my professional life because it revealed to me first-hand how occupation can change behavior as well as lives. It also gave me the opportunity to be a change agent even before I knew of the concept.

There were 15 residents living in a three-story converted mansion with no elevator. This type of facility would not be approved today for several reasons, but regulations were much more lenient and perhaps even non-existent back in 1971. Of the 15 residents, six elderly men occupied the third floor. Without an elevator, they limited their trips up and down the stairs to three times per day, for meals. The owner/administrator was concerned because they were all so angry. Not only were they verbally abusive to staff, they were openly hostile toward each other.

One of my responsibilities was to "get these men involved in something." I had no budget, supplies, or designated place to work, and I was limited to three hours per week. The third floor was a converted attic. The men lived in one large room that reeked of urine and body odor. They had an outside fire escape in case of emergency. I introduced myself to each man and interviewed them about their past occupations and interests. As I sat with each man I positioned myself to also watch what the other men were doing—which appeared to be nothing at all.

There was no TV. No one was reading or interacting with their neighbors. It seemed their only interest was in keeping track of time. They each had a wind-up clock and seemed very concerned about synchronizing the time with their neighbor's clocks, but without interaction.

Two of the men had radios, but they didn't listen to them. They just turned them on to check the time, and then shut them right off. There was complete silence as they sat on their beds, slept, or checked the time.

After my round of interviews, I suggested to the administrator that the men needed a work project. We brainstormed and came up with a project of making tissue boxes out of wooden kits. She agreed to pick up 20 of them so we could give one to each resident and have some for the offices. I asked her also to pick up extra sandpaper, two hammers, and some paintbrushes and paint. We decided that I would be the one to enlist the men's help with the project. I didn't want anyone to generate any unnecessary resistance that I may not be able to overcome.

I arrived at 9:30 a.m. the next Saturday, announced that the administrator had given me the job of making the tissue boxes, and asked for their help. Two men came over to see what I had in terms of supplies. I showed them a picture of a completed tissue box, and the assembly instructions that came with each kit. I had purposely brought a ball peen hammer with me from home knowing it was inappropriate for this type of work. They laughed when I brought it out and they loved being the expert in explaining why it was a claw hammer that was needed. These two men had some home maintenance or job experience using carpentry tools, and became my go-to guys for the work project.

So, with a large table set up, newspapers covering the table, tools at the ready, three kits opened up and we commenced to sanding our pieces. I learned that if I am working also, rather than just supervising, it is easier to interact. As we worked, I got them talking about the various options for finishing the boxes such as paint, stain, varnish or shellac. I purposely talked in a loud enough voice to be heard by the other men when I lamented that we had so much to do and that we needed to be done by the end of the month. This got two more to come join us. By the end of the morning I had all six sanding and hammering away.

I exaggerated my lack of knowledge in woodworking in order for them to become the decision-makers. They had some good ideas and some not so good, such as attaching the tissue boxes to the wall upside down so the tissues would always come out because of gravity.

I used my skills in group dynamics to turn this into a pretty effective task group. There were some differences of opinion, but I facilitated reasonable outcomes in each instance. It was surprising to me in that some of the six did not know each other's names, and they were surprised to learn that some of them had worked in the same place or lived near each other in the past. When my three hours were up I gathered up my stuff and placed everything in the closet next to the administrator's office.

When I arrived the following Saturday I received two pieces of good news. The first came from the administrator who said that the men asked all week when I was coming back and they wanted to know if they could work on the boxes without me. She explained that I was the person responsible for getting everything done right, and that she wanted them to wait for me. The other piece of good news came when I saw the men were all set up and ready to work by the time I reached their floor.

They worked cooperatively, shared the two claw hammers (I took the ball peen one back home) we had available and consulted with my two go-to guys. Though some friction between the men was still obvious, we were able to work together every Saturday morning until we completed the tissue boxes.

The administrator continued to come up with both the ideas and the funding for future projects. The work group came to be known as the Men's Club, and they built magazine racks, birdhouses, pencil holders, and other crafts. I moved on to help enhance other aspects of the activities program and left the men on their own.

Besides the reports from the staff of the men being more content and cooperative, I had my own observations of their engagement in the occupation of woodworking. This engagement in a meaningful occupation turned a collection of angry individuals into a somewhat harmonious team. The best evidence that this was successful was when I noticed that two of the clocks had stopped and no one seemed concerned.

22. An unusual request

"When life throws you lemons, make orange juice. It will leave them wondering how the hell you did that."
Author Unknown

As an occupational therapist in a skilled nursing and rehab facility I was often asked to assess residents who lived next door in a 22-story senior citizens apartment building. A resident in that complex made one of the more unusual requests that I had ever received, and put my problem solving, communication, and change agent skills to the test.

"Mr. Soar" was quite pleasant and coherent as I went through my assessment. He was 93 years old, a retired pharmacist and two-time widower. His strength, range of motion and coordination seemed fine, and I wondered why I was asked to see him. This puzzled me further as the assessment went on and he demonstrated he was able to take care of himself quite well, and had an amazing mind with intact cognition in all respects. Why was I here?

I got my answer when he said: "I know a little bit about OT because OTs and PTs often came into my pharmacy to look over the equipment we had for the handicapped. So, I know you OT folks know how to adapt things, and I need your help. Come out here."

We went out on his little balcony. Looking down from 21 floors was a little scary, but he was not bothered by the height. He turned to me and said calmly, "What I want you to do is to adapt a stool so I can get up and over this high railing. I have had a good life and am ready to soar off into the next life. Living here with all these handicapped, psychotic, and depressed people is depressing and I've had enough. So, will you help me?"

I, of course, was unsure of what to say, but I used a combination of interpersonal strategies with some success. I was very concerned about the well-thought out plan he had for committing suicide. I felt that as soon as I said I wouldn't help him, our conversation would be over and I would be asked to leave his home. He might then find some other way to implement his plan. So, I used validation in an unusual way. I said, "I am very impressed with your mind, and I can also understand why living here would not always be pleasant for you. Your rationale for dying is well-thought out, and I can see that you are a determined and well-organized person. I imagine all of these qualities served you well as a pharmacist and as a businessman."

These validating statements seemed to surprise and please him. He said, "This place is a madhouse, and if you weren't crazy when you moved in, you would be crazy in a short time." In response, I used my technique of "proposing the preposterous," and said, "I didn't realize that the whole population of this apartment tower had reached such a high level of dementia. Do you know if the Board of Trustees and the Health Department are aware of this? They certainly would need to know in order to perhaps start the process of re-classifying the facility from a senior citizens apartment complex to a nursing home."

It worked! He said, "Wait a minute. Just hold on. There are a lot of good people in here that are pretty smart. In fact, there are just a couple of bedbugs that get the rest of us all worked up. Don't go blabbing about what I said. That's all they need is to hear that now we're living in a nursing home, and that I instigated it."

To keep the relationship going (as I also thought about how I was going to handle all this,) I said, "Mr. Soar, I am curious as hell about something." He looked at me with interest. I said, "Many people who plan to kill themselves are often not deciding to die, but are coming to the conclusion that they do not want to live the life they are living. Does this fit your situation?" There seemed to be both comprehension and reflection on his face. He said, "Yes sir, you got it figured out pretty good! But, I still think the best thing for me is to soar."

I then came with the strongest piece of reality testing coupled with an attempt at reframing his situation. I said, "Look, let me give you three facts. Number one, both this building and the world are better off with you in it. Second, I'm not going to help you in any way to kill yourself, and third, my professional license and ethics dictate that I do my best to protect you from harm and that includes my letting the staff and your doctor know about all this. So, what do you think?"

It is at these times that our hearts beat faster and the need to use the bathroom is suddenly more urgent. However, I just waited patiently, kept my gaze on him and rubbed his shoulder to let him know I valued him as a person. It was pretty intense for a minute or so. Then he bent forward onto his knees and began to sob. It was very sad to see such a strong man crumble before me, but I knew this was ultimately a good thing.

When he had composed himself, I asked, "Who are the tears for?" He said, "I'm ashamed to say they are for me. I'm a mess." We then had a good conversation, with him going into more detail about how he felt his life was over, that there was no hope, and that he didn't know why he shouldn't just end it all. I ventured into reframing using what I call my magic wand. I said, "Go along with me on what may seem like a crazy and dumb idea, but it may help."

I handed him my pen and said, "Pretend that this pen is a magic wand and that you can change anything about your life in one stroke. Wave the magic wand and tell me what you would change." He was only hesitant for a moment and then he smiled and waved the "wand" while saying, "Put me back 40 years." He talked about his first wife, their five kids, their home, his pharmacy and store, his customers, grandkids, and so forth. He was clearly animated and joyful as he described his experiences. But, as he continued, he would tear up talking about how he had outlived two wives, three of his children, and a grandson.

I used validation again and showed genuine admiration for the life he had built. I talked with him about writing and living the next chapters of his life, but I had to be extremely direct to build a bridge with this very depressed man. What I said was, "You are really a fine person, and I think you are not done yet. We both know the 'magic wand' is just a way to get you to step back to get a different perspective. When we adopt a tunnel-vision perspective we often don't see any possibilities except one like suicide. What do you think about this?"

He did not answer quickly, but when he did he showed amazing insight. He said, "I see your point that I'm all twisted around. You coming here today is not what I expected to happen. That was stupid to think you would help me get over the railing. My kids and their kids would not have taken it well if you did."

The conversation became much more positive, but to be sure he was feeling differently I asked him to call one of his kids or grandkids

79

to set up a time to get together. He called his youngest daughter who lived about an hour away and she and her husband agreed to come take him out for lunch on Saturday (this was Thursday).

I left feeling that he was OK, and documented everything I could. I also called the social worker and the facility's administrator and explained what had taken place. Both promised to check in on Mr. Soar. I got to see him a few more times with informal visits, and could see he was taking on tasks to find new meaning in his life and keep himself rooted to this world.

The absence of meaningful occupations can be lethal as Mr. Soar almost demonstrated. I was unable to engage him in an occupation except for the occupation of living and re-investing in his family. These could be the precursors to engagement, or just his gaining a perspective on living rather than "soaring off into the next life."

23. From the Other Side

*"In the sick room, ten cents' worth of human understanding
equals ten dollars' worth of medical science."*
Martin H. Fischer (1879-1962)
German-American Physician

I have never been a recipient of OT, but I have been a patient of two different PTs (shoulder and knee), four different chiropractors, two podiatrists, several dentists, and three primary care physicians. Being a patient of these different healthcare providers has given me the perspective "from the other side" that has proven to be quite valuable. I also have the perspective of having accompanied several friends and family members to various medical appointments. In addition, I have worked alongside a multitude of OTs and other professionals in several practice arenas. All of these experiences has provided great learning for me, but I think the times I "was on the other side" with some of the pain, confusion, anxiety, and confusion that my patients experienced has proved the most valuable. Whether negative or positive I gained a valuable perspective, and experienced further insight into the helping relationship in terms of what is helpful and what is not. In other words, I learned how not to build a bridge, how not to listen, and essentially how not to be a change agent.

In spite of the negative examples I experienced, I have also witnessed exceptional skill and empathy in some healthcare providers, and these are my models. In the cases where I did not feel respected I still attempted to "build a bridge" with these providers, and to get what I needed from the relationships. I also attempted to educate them regardless of concerns that they might develop a negative perception of me and then do less for me in some way. I wonder how many of our patients have similar concerns about OT, but are hesitant to speak up? My two personal examples below are cases in point of what can happen when one does speak up.

The most recent experience occurred just this past winter when I woke with severe low back pain after driving several hours the day before. I was in Florida at the time and had to find a chiropractor and so started with the Yellow pages online. I called three who were booked, but then found one that was about 20 minutes from me that could see me. None of them accepted my health insurance so I knew that I would have to pay for this myself. It turned out that Tuesdays (this was a Tuesday) was a day that this office did paperwork and did not see patients, but they made an exception and agreed to see me. The receptionist was nice and I filled out all the paperwork. The Chiropractor was very good in that he really listened when I opposed his plan. He wanted to do x-rays and schedule me for three sessions per week. I'm thinking let's get it done today and I'll be on my way. Here is the dialogue:

"We have to do x-rays of your whole spine"

"Why?"

"To rule out cancer and other things"

"I think that's pretty remote because I have no other symptoms except my once-a-year S-I joint at S2 on my right that needs adjustment." Why can't you do what my Chiropractor does up north and see how it goes?"

"What does he do?"

I explained as best I could what modalities he used and the various positions and manipulations he performed, and he said: "OK, let's give that a try" (I was a bit surprised he "caved" so easily). He did his magic and I was on my way, and was fine. I was impressed that he listened and adjusted his thinking and his treatment plan to accommodate me.

Another example where I was not listened to until I used all my interpersonal skills to get a bridge built was with a PT. I was seeing him for a knee injury I sustained when I twisted it while helping my son move into his new house. The PT did not talk much, and when he did it was about his daughter, his house, his two dogs, and so forth. He had me on an exercise program that seemed to be working. I was able to get rid of the crutches and stop using the knee immobilizer, so I had confidence in him as a PT. However, the home exercise program he gave me was beyond what my pain level could tolerate, and so I couldn't complete them. Here is what the "big conversation" was like while I was standing in the parallel bars:

PT:"My dog Sabrina is getting so cute with my daughter. They just love each other, and are always looking to see where the other one is."

Me: "That home exercise program you gave seems to have been something "off the shelf" to fit all knee patients, and it's a problem for me."

PT: "Yeah, but that's one of our best protocols."

Me: "Really? It's killing me."

PT: "Stick with it. Hey Dave (another PT across the room), who do the Sabres play tonight? My wife got us tickets and I don't even know whose playing." (Loud laughter follows).

Me: I gesture to my PT to come closer with an intentionally serious look on my face. He says "What's the problem?" "You are not listening to me and I don't feel you respect me as a patient (confrontation). I think you have done very good work to get my knee to this point (validation), but you talk about things like your daughter, the Sabres, etc without listening to me."

PT: He looks at me. Good eye contact. Then he says, "I am sorry. I guess I was a little caught up with other things. Let's go through your home exercise program again and tell me where you are having problems."

Things were much different after that. My home program was modified, and I was back to full mobility and strength in 4 weeks. He thanked me at the end for talking to him honestly about how he was not listening to me.

What both these experiences have in common was how direct and confrontational I had to be to get what I wanted from these two healthcare providers. What if I had been less assertive? What would a less assertive person have gotten? Lots of x-rays, lots of Chiropractic appointments they didn't need, and a PT home exercise program that didn't work.

Since many of our patients are a bit intimidated when interacting with healthcare professionals, we as OTs have to ask, listen, and paraphrase to be sure the client's perspective is central to the treatment plan. We also have to monitor and ask on an ongoing basis things like:" What do you think of OT?" How is OT going for you? Is there anything you wish were different about OT"? By asking, listening, and paraphrasing we can know what adjustments to make to our interventions that are consistent with the client's needs and wants, and be the client-centered therapist we would like to be.

The foundation of the change agent relationship has to be active listening. It is through active listening that we truly discover the patient's perspective, and just as importantly, demonstrate our respect for our patients.

24. Respect is returned in kind

"When we treat people merely as they are, they will remain
as they are. When we treat them as if they were what they
should be, they will become what they should be."
Thomas S. Monson (1927—)
American religious leader

**Figure 24-1. The benefits of treating people with respect can have
a great yield.**

When working as the head of occupational therapy in a large
skilled-nursing facility, I decided to take advantage of a new
program that was being initiated. Our OT department would take
part in what was known as the *welfare-to-work program*. The way the
program worked was that those receiving public assistance would be
assigned to work at the various county facilities, and we could have
people to help us with the task of patient transportation, which had
been eating into our productivity. This facility was spread out over
three quarters of a mile with the OT room located on the opposite
end from the patients. If we could have a real patient transportation
system using these workers, we therapists could spend more time
providing OT.

This was my first time as a department head and I was quite
young. My colleagues told me things like, "You're crazy. These people
don't want to work. They will steal us blind." None of it mattered. I
was going forward.

The person running this program for the county was pleased
to have what he called "a taker." Apparently, few agencies were
willing to take a chance and participate. The program required that
all able-bodied people receiving public assistance who did not have

childcare responsibilities work in one of the county agencies or facilities. The number of required workdays varied from five to 15. Since the people enrolled in the program did not have cars and our facility was 26 miles from the city, their only means of transportation was a school bus provided by the county.

I really saw this as an opportunity to give people a chance to work in a supportive environment while also providing needed services for my patients. When the program began the following week, I was determined to treat each new worker with dignity and respect, and asked my staff to do the same. The first thing I did was to instruct my staff to stop using the term *welfare* and say *public assistance* instead. Just saying the word *welfare* would have perpetuated the negative associations people have about public assistance.

I interviewed each person to find out what work they had done, their skills and the kind of work they would like to do. I promised each of them that if they came to work as scheduled and worked hard, acted in a professional manner, and interacted with our patients in a kind and respectful way, I would write them a letter of recommendation. I felt people in this situation may not have many letters of recommendation and such a letter on official letterhead could enhance their employability.

I also got each one a name tag that identified them as members of the Occupational Therapy Department, and they all took pride in wearing them. They chose the name they preferred on the tag as well as how they would like to be addressed. Some were fine with their first names, some had nicknames, and some preferred the more formal addresses of Mr., Mrs., etc.

The first person they sent us had been a secretary and had good interpersonal skills. She was our first patient transporter, a title I chose deliberately because I thought it had more status than porter or transport aide.

She worked as a patient transporter in the morning and our secretary/receptionist in the afternoon. She was very personable and her interpersonal skills helped me get this program going. The patients and nursing staff really liked her. The next two workers sent to us were also very dependable and conscientious. The patients loved them and always asked when they were coming back.

The program quickly grew to the point that we had enough patient transporters for continuous coverage, and our own secretary. Around this time, some of the other department heads approached me about my getting them what they called "those welfare people." The program thus expanded into Housekeeping, Laundry, and Activities. At full swing up to 30 people a day worked at our facility, one full busload.

We had our occasional mishaps (people not showing, coming in with the smell of alcohol, being argumentative, etc.) but we had far more success stories. Eventually, I had our first person become our secretary/receptionist as her full-time duty—a position she loved. One worker was hired full-time in Housekeeping and was able to get off public assistance. I wrote many letters of recommendation.

This story still stands out: One young man, I discovered in our interview, had been a history teacher and had earned a master's degree. After a short time he proved to be one of our best. He had a gentle way about him. I asked if he was still interested in teaching and we decided to explore the creation of a school within our facility, with approval from our administrator. The local school district donated books and some teaching supplies.

A vacant room in the new wing of the facility became a classroom for patients who wanted to earn their G.E.D., learn to read or write, become more knowledgeable about a subject like history, or just brush up on their spelling. Our teacher created a wonderful learning environment, and the numbers of students grew to 11.

Eventually the teacher came to me to say that he realized how he missed his work as a teacher and that he was going to apply for a position at one of the area schools. He got the job. With his leaving I thought we were going to have to close the school, but one of the OTAs was also a former elementary school teacher who was interested in teaching rather than OT. I approached the administrator and he approved a transfer. She ran the school for another year, until her retirement.

Due to funding and legal issues the Department of Social Services had to discontinue this worthwhile program after just one year of operation. While the program lasted, our patients' lives were definitely enriched, our OT program flourished, and a lot of people had the opportunity to be treated with respect and dignity.

At the time I didn't know it, but I was doing change agent work on a larger scale than I realized. Giving people the opportunity to work was the antidote to any occupational alienation that may have been present. A corollary was attitudes of a number of employees were changed as they were able to dispel old stereotypes about "those welfare people."

Part III:

Career Steps, Missteps, and Learning:

"Do what you can, with what you have, where you are."
Theodore Roosevelt (1858-1919)
26th President of the United States of America

25. Finding and capturing the best OT job

"The secret of being miserable is to have the leisure to bother about whether your or happy or not. The cure is occupation."
George Bernard Shaw (1856-1950)
Critic, Playwright, and Essayist

Today, new graduates can take advantage of the high demand for OTs in some cities, but must also be ready to compete in areas where there is an ample supply of therapists and limited positions. Moving into the job market from the classroom is a big change, as is the change in jobs after you decide to move on. Regardless, whether it's your first job or jobs in your future this information can make the change more fluid and successful. Certainly, students completing a level II fieldwork or internship usually have the inside track. However, a new graduate searching for a position in another facility or even unfamiliar city needs to gain an advantage over their peers.

Having recently been through the search process myself and numerous times in the past I have gained some insights that can be useful. In addition, as a former manager and owner of a private practice, I have probably interviewed more than 300 prospective OTRs and COTAs myself. All of these experiences have resulted in a compendium of ideas that I usually share in a workshop for students departing from Keuka College that I now offer here for future graduates and those considering a change in jobs.

The strategies vary with the stage of the job search for each person. Students may be surprised to learn that the job search actually can start and end at the student's first level II fieldwork experience. As a fieldwork supervisor, I always looked at students as potential employees depending how well they performed. The time spent training during fieldwork can pay dividends because there is far less time needed to reach competence once they are hired. Other supervisors also know this well, so take heed.

If you want to expedite the search process in a new geographic or even into a new clinical area, consider using a recruiter. They usually

91

have jobs that don't get advertised and they charge the employer, not you the employee. You can post your resume with any number of them and see what they produce. I just posted my resume' with four services in southwest Florida, and was pleased with the response.

Recruiters got a bad name a few years back because they placed new graduates in challenging situations without proper supervision. The good recruiting companies now provide supervision and a mentor for new graduates, and this is something you can also negotiate. The recruiter screens applicants and then recommends them to employers who contract with the recruiting agency for their services.

I have also been exploring traveling therapy and I have been very impressed with their salaries and benefit packages. Some provide housing and others provide a housing stipend. Add this to tuition reimbursement, sign-on bonuses, paid licensing, and it's a pretty good deal for those geographically mobile. You also get to pick where you want to go. They often provide some supervision and an online mentor. You must sign on for three-month stints, but you can take time off in between without pay.

A good way to learn firsthand whether or not traveling therapy is for you is to ask your contact person for names and email addresses or even phone numbers of OTs (PTs won't be as relevant) that have been with the company for at least a year. Then, contact them to find out what it is really like as a traveling therapist.

Assuming you want to find the job on your own and prefer not to travel or use a recruiter, then these ideas will help you be successful. First, do your homework. Pick the population you want to work with and the part of the country that appeal to you. Then, scour the Internet and publications like *OT Advance* and *OT Practice* for possible job leads. You need to prepare two resume's, each just one page in length. One is what I call a *generic resume'*, that you can quickly send off to any job lead. The second is a *targeted resume'* that highlights your specific qualifications for a job you found advertised. The *targeted resumes'* are structured around the advertisement's requirements, and how your education and experiences match. Remember, the purpose of the resume' is not to get the job, but to get an interview. It's during the interview where you sell yourself and hopefully get the job offer.

In terms of references, don't include them. Employers are not impressed with letters of high praise that a candidate sends or brings to an interview. The best thing to do is to have a list of clinicians who have supervised you and all of their contact information available at the interview. You will be a much stronger candidate if you have clinicians who have seen you work with clients rather than professors who only know your academic work or ministers who say you are a great churchgoer. Your resume' can simply say: References available upon request.

Whether you send your resume' as an attachment or through the mail, you need to include a brief cover letter. Remember, the purpose of the cover letter is to get the potential employer to look at your resume'. These letters are short and have a sentence or two that causes the employer to look over your resume'.

As part of your research on the agency or facility you can check out the facility's website (most have one), and include a sentence or two that shows your same commitment to their stated mission or values. Or, another approach is to state something about how the work you did on one of your clinical experiences is in sync with their clients' needs.

You want everything you send to a prospective employer to be very professional. This means, no errors in grammar or spelling. Make it easy for them to contact you by having all of your phone numbers and email addresses right at the top. You may want to consider changing your email address if is something like ptaltypartyguy. yahoo. This also applies to your rock or rap music that greets people on your voicemail.

In a competitive job market you have to be ready to follow up. Give them a week or so to respond, and then call or email them to see if they received your resume'. Within this same conversation restate your strong interest in the position and availability for an interview at their convenience. This is also an appropriate time to ask how soon they expect to make their decision. Do not ask about salary or benefits during this conversation. This happens later when they make the job offer.

Having interviewed hundreds of OTs over the years I have some specific suggestions on how to get a job offer from an interview:

- Arrive early and be prepared to wait patiently. Bring something to read or work on, and then you won't be as annoyed if you have to wait a long time. It also gives the impression that you are an organized and productive person.

- Stand and shake hands with the person who is going to interview you. Make it a firm handshake (not bone-crushing but firm), make good eye contact, and say the person's name.

- Remember that most people looking to hire an OT are trying to figure out how you stack up on what I call *the 4 Cs*: Cooperation, Compatibility, and Clinical Competence. So, as you answer their questions, be thinking of ways to weave examples of how you are strong in each of these *4Cs*.

- Show that you took the time to do research on the facility and how your education and clinical experience matches their clients' needs.

- Most interviews are about 45 minutes long, and the skills of interviewers vary greatly. Some don't shut up enough to give you a chance to talk, and others are not sure what questions to ask you. In any event be ready to be forthright and ask questions about the client's needs, the program's resources, the potential for new program development, support for continuing education, and so forth.

- The questions not to ask are those that are self-serving like your salary, pay raises, vacation time, health insurance, etc. They will provide this information when they make the job offer.

- In many cases, such as governmental organizations, the salary is not negotiable, but if they have some flexibility they may ask you what kind of salary you are looking to receive. A good response is to say that you didn't get into OT because of the money (which is true for most of us), and so the salary is not as important as the opportunity to do good clinical work and to grow in the job professionally, or something to this effect.

• When the interview ends shake hands once again and restate your strong interest in the position.

Send the person who interviewed you a brief hand-written thank-you card. Thank them for their time and emphasize some aspect of the facility or the OT program that impressed you during the interview. This shows that you are an observant and perceptive candidate and someone they want to hire. If you were interviewed by other people involved in the hiring decision, send them a thank you card also.

I have been disappointed and impressed by how people react during an interview. Remember, the resume' gets you the interview, and the interview will hopefully get you the job offer. In the next chapter you can read about mistakes I have seen in interviews.

26. Interview Missteps: bare midriffs, German Shepherds and spouses

"Never wear a backward cap to an interview unless applying for the job of umpire." Dan Zevin,
American Author

In 1972, I once interviewed 85 COTAs for one position. This was my first time as a supervisor and I didn't know to screen people out based on their resume's. It was also a time when there was a large surplus of COTAs in the Buffalo area because the program at Erie Community College was very popular and graduated 60 students per year with limited local job prospects. So, when I ran my ad, 85 submitted resumes—all were new or recent graduates. Since they all seemed equally qualified, and no one told me any different, I thought I needed to do a face-to-face interview with all of them.

It was a crazy time with interviewing in between doing patient evaluations and treatments, while also supervising a busy OT department. However, I learned so much about interviewing—about people and how the interviewing process is so stressful that people do the strangest things. For example, one person went behind my desk and sat down. I was shocked but didn't want to embarrass her and generate more stress, so I sat in a side chair across from her. The conversation was proceeding nicely until a PT friend stopped by and said jokingly, "Did you lose your job Peter or get a new boss?" The girl understood immediately and jumped up apologizing profusely. We laughed a lot about it and continued the interview in the appropriate chairs.

I recognized early on that the interview process, especially for a newbie, is challenging because some people are extremely verbal and others are so shy that they can only give one or two word answers. I didn't know that my mental health background was going to be so useful. Getting rambling talkers to focus was as difficult as getting terrified people to speak in sentences.

One person answered every question with a question and in a hostile manner. When asked why she became a COTA, she said, "What business is that of yours?" She didn't get the job. Nor, did I hire the non-stop talking woman who disclosed details about her personal life and values without any restraint. The person I did hire for this position was a disaster and left by her choice after only a few weeks. I did better with my second choice and she stayed 20 years. I was gone in three years, but I took with me the skills of interviewing and hiring that helped me in subsequent positions.

One of the key areas that can often be determined through an interview is the candidate's judgment. The practice of OT in every setting requires intact judgment and decision making. So, in the category of "what were they thinking?" what caused one candidate to bring her pet German Shepherd dog to the interview in a school district? It did not help that the dog didn't like me. Any movement brought out a growl.

Then there were the people who brought a parent, spouse, boyfriend, etc., with them, and who insisted on sitting in on the interview. Sometimes it was the candidates themselves who asked for this. What does this say about independence, confidence, and judgment? Some of these guests sat quietly during the interview and others prompted and even answered on behalf of the candidate. One boyfriend said that my questions were biased toward experienced therapists, and advised his girlfriend not to answer them.

Dress was another surprising choice. An OTR male candidate dressed in a three-piece suit complete with cufflinks. He looked and acted like he was applying for an attorney or CEO position. The opposite occurred too. Some did not put any effort into their appearance, wearing jeans, a tank top, or shorts.

Provocative dress that befits a night on the town was always baffling. Some job candidates wore low-cut dresses, no bra, or had their mid-drifts visible with navel jewelry. Did they think that dressing in a seductive way would get them the job? Not where I work and am responsible for the actions of the people I hire.

Once, I called a person for an interview because the man had noted on his application that he had volunteered in our department five years earlier to complete his admission requirements for OT school. He surprised me by walking into my office wearing a nice dress, high heels, a wig, and full make-up. It was evident that he took time to present himself in a professional manner.

But, I guess my confusion was obvious, as I kept glancing back at his male name on his resume'. I had learned enough about employment law to know that transgendered people are part of protected classes, so I was careful not to break the law and ask illegal questions. He volunteered that he was "exploring his gender identity," and felt that occupational therapy was a sensitive and unbiased profession in which he/she could do this.

He was poised, articulate, bright, and had a good grasp of OT at an entry-level. I explained the responsibilities that went with the position and that he would be half-time school-based and half-time home health. He did not like the dual responsibilities and the considerable travel required, and so he thanked me for my time and left.

I think he could have been a good addition to our staff, but I always wondered if he would have encountered confusion or disrespect. And, would I have endangered some contracts because of the image he presented? Or, would his interpersonal and clinical skills over-ride any concerns our clients and agency personnel might have had? I never heard where he ended up working and how it all worked out, but that was an interview I will always remember.

The best way to hone your interviewing skill, besides avoiding some of the obvious mistakes above, is to practice. Throughout my career I always believed that the best time to look for a new job is when you don't need one. Going through the interview process helps you see different interview styles, and you can try out different responses to questions and assess the impact.

This approach led me to be interviewed in well over 100 positions in nine states and two Canadian provinces over 42 years as an OT. The positions ranged from staff therapists, OT directors, rehabilitation coordinators, professors, program managers, consultants, vice-presidents, and even the director of a mental health facility. I have been interviewed by people at all levels of an organization, by teams, by consumers, and by the people I was expected to supervise and develop.

From every interview I learned something that has helped me when I was doing the interviewing, and when I went on subsequent interviews which I am still doing. So, go out and cultivate interviews throughout your professional life. Just don't bring your dog.

27. Getting fired is not the end

"I am still in shock and in awe of being fired."
Peter Arnett (1934—)
New Zealand-American journalist

In 1969, I began my OT career. After considering several offers, I decided to work in mental health and accepted a job at a large local hospital in the mental health division of the OT department. I was assigned to a team in an acute psychiatric unit where the average length of stay was 11 days. This was during the community mental health movement, and the intent was to develop and use community resources to prevent long-term institutionalization. It was exciting work, and I loved the team to which I was assigned.

But in less than a year, I began to get disillusioned—not with the work, but with the administration. My boss, though a great clinician, was not the best administrator and seemed to have little time for her staff. Who could do her job better, I thought, than me? It didn't help my ego that the COTAs who worked with me thought that I was the best thing that ever happened to them, and I was well liked and respected by my team. It turned out that we were all crazy!

My boss not only had to be the primary OT for a mental health team, but was also responsible for the five COTAs working in mental health, the six OTs working in physical disabilities on the acute care side of the hospital, and three more OTs working at a school on the hospital grounds for children with developmental disabilities. Clearly, she needed help with running the day-to-day aspects of the mental-health team.

Initially, I had good intentions. I became an informal senior therapist running things. But I began making decisions without consulting her. I called meetings, reassigned staff, changed job descriptions, tried to get the staff raises, wrote memos, and so forth. Naturally, these independent actions produced great conflict between my boss and me. In her view, I was out of control. In my mind, I was saving the OT department.

After six months of this craziness, my boss called me in on Dec. 1st of 1969 and fired me. She was nice about it, and said that if I resigned she would give me a good recommendation. I responded in my usual dumb and immature way and explained that she couldn't really fire me because my team and the COTAs loved me.

I left her office and went to see the two psychiatrists who jointly ran the team to which I was assigned. They took my case to the department of human resources. But the human resources director told me I really was fired.

Being fired from my first OT job was surely a 2x4 in the face. I couldn't believe it because I had convinced myself that I was the best OT ever.

After a frustrating job search, I found work at a large skilled nursing facility. The facility was outside of Buffalo and luckily for me outside of the OT grapevine. The interview went well, my previous boss gave me a good recommendation, as promised, and I got the job. It turned out to be a great new beginning.

The facility was large with 640 patients spread out in several connected buildings. It was almost equally divided between assisted living and skilled nursing. My boss was a physical therapist who had been there for 17 years and had a very positive view of occupational therapy, as did the administrator. They actually built an office for me, and gave me five former nurse's aides who were running several crafts programs that created goods sold in the gift shop. My job was to create the OT program with the staff assigned. I loved the bigness of the whole thing.

The patient population was diverse in age and diagnosis. There was a cluster of young people with spinal cord injuries, cerebral palsy, Down syndrome, blindness, and so forth. Older patients tended to have strokes, Parkinson's, arthritis, dementia, schizophrenia, amputations, MS, and rare conditions like syringomyelia, in which a cyst or cavity forms in the spinal cord.

I evaluated patients, and then taught the nurse's aides to carry out the treatment programs. It wasn't the best way to do OT, but the staff was very motivated and capable of following my direction. Two of the aides went to Erie Community College and became COTAs, and we were able to get two additional COTA positions to make us a legitimate OT program.

The main facility was renovated, and I was able to order all new equipment for a modern OT program. I established relationships with UB and Erie Community College so that fieldwork students were a part of our program, and I became a frequent guest speaker in their OT programs. This got me very interested in doing clinical as well classroom teaching.

The opportunity to build an OT program from the bottom up may not have occurred so early on in my career if I had not been fired. This experience over three years enabled me to apply for and obtain the position as chief occupational therapist at the Loretto Geriatric Center (now known as the Loretto Center) in Syracuse.

I once again got to build an OT program from the bottom up, hire and supervise five OTRs and a COTA, and establish a dynamic program. This experience led to my being recruited to come back to Buffalo and take a joint position as assistant clinical professor at the University of Buffalo, and head up the OT program at the Erie County Medical Center which was the same facility that I had been fired from six years earlier.

The woman who fired me had left several years earlier, and most of the OT staff was new. I ended up then moving from the joint position to a full-time academic position at UB.

Yes, being fired from my first OT job was traumatic, but it led to something amazing. The firing put me on a path where I developed sound clinical skills with diverse conditions, and became an effective leader and teacher. It may have been less painful to gain these skills without being fired, but I needed the "2x4 in the face" to rein in my ego and get me on the rewarding path I found.

28. Give second chances

"The weak can never forgive. Forgiveness is the attribute of the strong."
Mahatma Gandhi (1869-1948)
Leader of Indian nationalism in British-ruled India

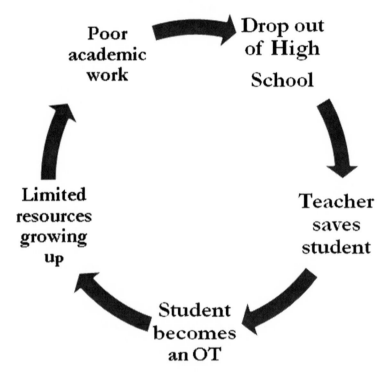

Figure 28-1. A second chance that worked out quite well.

I was not a good student in grammar school and even worse in high school. Because of my poor academic performance the teachers and guidance counselor in grammar school encouraged me to pursue a trade and I chose to become a baker.

I lasted three years at Emerson Vocational High School, but left at the end of my junior year knowing that I would not be able to finish the baking program. I tried to get a job at several large industrial plants and all of the utility corporations, but was told that without a high school diploma they would not consider hiring me. Fortunately, I was able get a job as a janitor in a school because my uncle was the engineer.

After two years of boring and unrewarding work and no better prospects I decided to return to high school. I discovered that not far from where I worked was a high school completion program. It wasn't a GED, but regular high school courses leading to a diploma. I started off with three courses: World History, General Science, and a Bookkeeping course as an elective.

Each course met for one hour three nights per week. If I took three courses each semester, at the end of two years I would have my high school diploma. I was getting a second chance. However, an incident occurred in the second week of the Bookkeeping class that almost made me drop out for a second time.

But let me back up. The Bookkeeping class was interesting to me because I had never learned about how a business ran with balance sheets, ledgers, debits, credits, and so forth. We had to buy a packet that contained all the bookkeeping materials for a small business. It was my first class each night, and I had little confidence in myself as a student but the structure of the course was helping.

The course was taught in a large study hall. It had about 50 old desks with the tops that flip up, so you can put your stuff in it. Only 15 students were in the course. Most were about 15 or 16 years of age while I was the old man of 18. I kept to myself and just did my work because the other students were too immature for me.

On this particular night I arrived early, put all of my books on my usual desk. Four or five students were gathered near my desk near the front of the room talking and laughing as usual. Also, as usual I ignored them and they me. I took my bookkeeping workbook and went to the bathroom. When I returned all of my books were gone. I tried asking the group of students, but they were all laughing and would not look at me or even respond.

I then started to search each of the 50 vacant desks flipping up the tops to see if the immature students had hid them. I was methodically checking each desk when the teacher came in to start class.

He told me to sit down, that the class was going to start. I tried to explain that I had to find my books. He yelled, "SIT DOWN!"

103

I just about ran to the front of the room, yelled, "#%@$# you!" to the teacher, and threw my bookkeeping workbook in the wastebasket. That was the end of my academic career for sure.

When I got home and announced to my family that I quit, they were not surprised. My parents said, "at least you have a job. Don't mess that up." Their response was to be expected because I had such a bad performance record throughout grammar and high school. I was despondent.

The next day it was back to the mop. I would be a career janitor, it seemed. Then, my uncle, who was also my boss, interrupted my mopping to tell me I had a phone call. He scolded me for getting a call in the workplace, even though it was the first one in my two years there.

So, I went down to the office with anxiety about my family being hurt or something tragic. It was my Bookkeeping teacher. He called my home and got my work number from my mom. I will always remember his exact words: "Peter, this is Mr. _____ from night school and I want to apologize for last night. I didn't know what was going on when I told you to sit down. After you left, the girls in front told me that they hid your books as a joke. I have your books right here, and if you can come to the next class a half hour earlier I can catch you up on what you missed." I said, "I'll be there." This was another second chance!

I went back to school, earned great grades and received my high school diploma all because my teacher gave me that second chance. I surprised myself in doing so well in school, and began to tentatively consider going to college. The University at Buffalo has a night-school branch where I enrolled and started taking courses. Three years, later I changed my major from anthropology to occupational therapy, and transferred into the day school at UB.

Now, fast forward to 1988 where, in addition to serving as the chair of OT at Keuka College, I owned and operated an OT private practice with 30 therapists providing occupational therapy to schools, hospice, nursing homes, home health, day treatment programs for adults with developmental disabilities and mental health programs in the eight counties of western New York. Under that structure, I had a few places where I practiced occupational therapy, and one of them was a skilled nursing facility.

One day at this facility, I received a referral to evaluate a man who was admitted after sustaining a stroke. The name was the same as my old Bookkeeping teacher. Could it be the same guy who 28 years ago gave me that wonderful second chance?

I went to see him and began the evaluation. Fortunately, his stroke had been mild and he had good return except for some deficits in grip strength and fine dexterity. As we chatted I could tell that his cognition was intact. I then said to him, "Are you by any chance the Mr. _____that taught Bookkeeping in 1960 at the Bennett High School evening program?"

Once he confirmed that he was, I then told him the story of how his phone call to me offering the second chance changed my life. He listened closely as I explained what came from his good work. He then said something else that I will never forget: "Forgive me if I don't remember your specific situation, but I did that type of thing a lot throughout my teaching career because that's what I think teachers should do."

I got to work with him on a few occasions, and then he was discharged to home. I would like to think I was able to return the favor by giving him a second chance, but as it turned out he didn't need it. He functioned well enough to return to home on his own. It didn't matter because I was able to thank the man in person who helped me start on a very rewarding path.

Throughout my career I have witnessed first-hand the benefits of giving people second chances. I have hired therapists who had been fired from other companies, and taken on students for Level II Fieldwork experiences who were unsuccessful in their prior placement.

Working in a substance abuse program I saw this second-chance concept on numerous occasions. Twelve-step programs like Alcoholics Anonymous and Narcotics Anonymous never give up on people. They see every person as having the potential to overcome their addictions and achieve sobriety regardless of the duration or extent of their addiction.

I remember one man who had gone through detoxification 34 times. I was impressed with how the counselors treated him with the same respect and optimism every time just as if he were being admitted for the first time. He did eventually see the light and engage in the recovery process.

Do second, third, and even 34 chances always work out? Do some people take advantage of these opportunities and manipulate others to their advantage? Yes, yes, and yes, but not to the extent that many people think.

In my experience, people who have made mistakes and then experienced the adverse consequences are usually remorseful and sometimes even desperate. I can elicit this in talking with them, and assess their level of insight about their errors. If they are vehemently blaming others and taking little responsibility for their situation, then the second chance may be wasted. However, this is seldom the situation. Most people given second chances make the most of them. I did.

29. When the shoe doesn't fit

For every failure, there is an alternative course of action. You just have to find it. When you come to a roadblock, take a detour."
Mary Kay Ash (1918-2001)
American businesswoman and founder of Mary Kay Cosmetics, Inc.

I have had a lifelong problem that existed for many years before it was resolved through perseverance, creativity, divine intervention, and/or luck, depending on your point of view. It had to do with my feet.

I was born with a clubfoot known as talipes equinovarus. My ankle and foot instead of being at 90 degrees, was pointed downward and inwards. It was surgically corrected when I was an infant with what is known as a triple arthrodesis. The foot was set at 90 degrees and fused. It gave me a stable ankle and I could walk, run, and jump with no problem.

The only problem I had was that the foot was stunted in its growth. As an adult the difference is now four sizes. I wear a size 13 on the left and a 9 on the right. As a kid I was supposed to be wearing high orthopedic shoes, but they were ugly and my family couldn't afford them. So, they would buy two pairs of sneakers and I would stuff the toe in one. This worked fairly well, but was not the best solution.

When I reached adulthood and could buy my own shoes, I bought one pair of special orthopedic shoes. However, for sneakers I still had to buy two pairs. I never knew what to do with other pair. What did Goodwill do with all the mismatched pairs I gave them over the years? I suspect there was more than one confused recipient out there stuffing the toes.

One day, when I saw an ad in *OT Advance* about a therapist in Phoenix who started a computer search service called "The Odd Shoe Exchange," it struck a chord. Her idea was to match people with amputations by shoe size so they could exchange footwear, provided, of course, the amputations were on opposite feet. I filled out the information on my sizes and paid my $25 registration fee.

It turned out that because of the lengths and widths of my feet she couldn't find a match. I went back to stuffing toes.

But, as you know by now, I have believed throughout my life that no problem is without a solution and I never give up. So I wrote a classified ad and placed it in the personals column of the *Buffalo News*. It said:

> *Man with two different size feet (Right 9 and Left 13) seeking man with opposite sizes for the purpose of sharing cost of shoes. Please call . . .*

At first, I did not receive any response except from a shoe salesman who wanted to sell me two pairs. Then good fortune struck. A local newscaster read my ad as a humorous way to end his TV show. A viewer ended up combing through her old newspapers, found my ad, and called her son who happened to live about 15 minutes from where I lived.

It turned out that this gentleman had polio as a child, which stunted the growth of one of his feet in a way that was the opposite of mine. We got together and found that we matched perfectly.

That was over 40 years ago and we have been shoe-buddies ever since. At the time we met, I was playing a lot of basketball and he was a tennis player. We were thus able to share the cost of sneakers. Then we expanded into boots, rubbers, dress shoes, moccasins, Crocs, slippers, etc. We never had it so good when it came to footwear. Around 10 years after we met we both started distance running and then changed to buying running shoes together.

My shoe-buddy's daughter was a journalism major in college. She wrote about us and was able to get the story published in *Runners' World* magazine. Not long after it appeared, my friend got a phone call from a freelance writer who wanted to write something more in-depth. We agreed because the whole thing was fun and we wanted to share it. The writer told us that he was going to send it to numerous places but had no idea where it would end up.

A friend called me a few weeks later to say that our story with our picture was in the *National Enquirer*. I went right out to the grocery store and bought 20 copies for my friends and family.

We are still exchanging shoes today. He and I are the same age, and he says that "whichever one of dies first, the survivor will be the loudest mourner at the funeral wailing loudly in the back of the church."

What did I learn from all this? Whether it's perseverance, creativity, divine intervention or luck, pursue your crazy dreams—in occupational therapy and in life, on behalf of your patients, your family and yourself. You never know when your life will be made richer by finding a perfect match.